A PILGRIM IN CELTIC SCOTLAND

To Nuala C. Begley
Dundalk
who taught me computer science

John J. Ó Ríordáin, CSSR

A Pilgrim
in
Celtic Scotland

the columba press

First published in 1997 by
the columba press
55a Spruce Avenue, Stillorgan Industrial Park,
Blackrock, Co Dublin

Cover by Bill Bolger
Cover photographs by the author
Origination by The Columba Press
Printed in Ireland by Colour Books Ltd, Dublin

ISBN 1 85607 193 6

Acknowledgements

English quotations from St Adamnán's *Life of Columcille* are by Dr Daniel J. McCarthy, Bishop of Kerry. The excerpt from *Liber de mensura orbis terrae* is used with permission of The Royal Irish Academy. The poem, *Cormac the Sailor* is from *The Wreck of the Archangel*, by George Mackay Brown, published by John Murray Publishers, London.

Contents

Foreword

For much of each year I live out of a suitcase. My journeys as an itinerant missioner have taken me not only all over Ireland but further afield, including North America, Continental Europe and especially Scotland. The following pages are about Scotland, specifically aspects of Celtic Scotland. The 'Scotland' of which I write is not confined to the political entity of either today or yester-year. It is an indefinitely bounded spiritual country stretching from Lindisfarne to the Faroe Islands and from the Atlantic Ocean to the North Sea.

Over the years I have visited and revisited the places of which I write, not just to work, not simply as a tourist, but in the deeper way of the pilgrim, caught up in that same tradition that inspired such people as Columcille of Derry and Iona, Brendan the Navigator and Cormac the Sailor to seek out places most congenial to the pursuit of a life with both depth and meaning. It is my hope, therefore, that this book will not only be an informative resource for visitors, but an invitation to move from tourist to pilgrim and return home more enriched for that experience. For this reason, I have added at the end a chapter on Christian pilgrimage and another containing prayers suited to such an undertaking.

I am much indebted to my confrères Dick Tobin and Louis G. Eustace, CSsR, and to Helen McCarthy of Limerick for a veriety of helpful insights and suggestions relating to the text, and to Sarah and Leslie Dreever of Kirkwall for ensuring that I got to the Brough of Deerness. My special thanks to the people of the Outer Hebridean islands of Eriskay, South Uist, Benbecula and Barra, among whom I spent most time and who gave me a truly Gaelic welcome; but also to the many people all over mainland and islands, be they friendly helpers, bus-drivers, sailors, inn-keepers, clergy, the household of the Cathedral presbytery in Oban, and others who facilitated me along my pilgrim way. Finally, I can never think of those outings to Scotland without recalling so many wonderful and entertaining memories of Margaret King, Evelyn Geraghty, Carmel O'Keeffe, Clement McManus, Mary Clare Moriarty, Marian Short and Joseph Naughton, each of whose temperament and personality made for ideal pilgrim companionship. In all your travels may you meet with the hospitality encouraged by the eighth-century *Rule of St Ailbe* – a clean house, a big fire, a good wash and comfortable bed.

John J. Ó Ríordáin, CSSR,
St Joseph's,
Dundalk,
Co Louth,
Ireland.
Feast of St Ninian, 1996.

Introduction

About eight thousand year ago, some enterprising Mesolithic (Middle Stone Age) people set out on a voyage over the North Channel from Stranraer in Scotland to Larne in Ireland and since then the traffic on that route has never ceased. It has influenced both countries over the millennia, but in this book I am concentrating on the influence it has had on Scotland. During that time, Scotland was influenced from other sources, notably southern Britain, Scandinavia and Rome. Readers unfamiliar with these cultural, political, religious and demographic influences on Scotland may find in these introductory pages a useful, if condensed, underlay which is taken-for-granted throughout the rest of the book.

From the time immediately prior to the Christian era, Imperial Rome turned its eyes to Britain. At that time, Britons peopled the island from the Clyde to the English Channel, while the northern part of the island was occupied by various groupings of Picts ('painted people') as the Romans called them. Julius Caesar invaded Britain in 55 BC, but a considerable time elapsed before the island became a full province of the empire. And even then, the province did not include the whole island because the Romans failed to subdue the Pictish people in the northern mountains and glens of Scotland.

To defend the northern borders against the Picts, Hadrian ordered the construction of a massive rampart, *Hadrian's Wall*. It was built about AD 122-26, and ran from Wallsend on the Tyne estuary to Bowness on the Solway Firth, a distance of seventy-three English miles. Less than a generation later, Antoninus Pius (138-61) built another wall, this time further north, between the Forth and Clyde, and it, too, took its name from the emperor – the *Antonine Wall*.

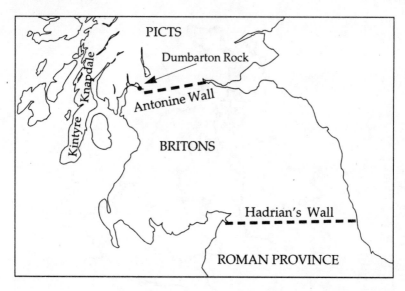

In Roman times, the Britons of Strathclyde maintained a little kingdom of their own, with its capital at Dumbarton Rock. Its boundaries varied with the fortunes of war but generally kept within the two Roman walls. Being north of Hadrian's Wall, these Britons were outside the Roman province, but close enough to be influenced by it. At times, the Romans had defensive settlements within the kingdom of Strathclyde, and it may well have been cultivated as a buffer state between the empire and the dreaded Picts further north.

Turning from the Romans to the Irish, we find that about the end of the third century AD, an Irish adventuring contingent, under the leadership of Cairbre Riada, moved north from west Munster to east Ulster and carved out for themselves a little kingdom on the Antrim coast known in tradition as *Dal Riada*, the territory of (Cairbre) Riada. About a century later, Irish people from Dal Riada began to drift across the North Channel into the south west of Scotland. The area occupied by these settlers became known as the district of the *Gallgaedhil* ('foreign Irish') from which the name 'Galloway' is derived. Nor were the descendants of Cairbre Riada content to stay at home there either. They expanded their kingdom into the regions of Kintyre and Knapdale under the title *'Scottish Dal Riada.'*

At the end of the fifth century, the west coast of Scotland was sub-jected to yet another incursion of Gaels from Ireland. This band was Christian and led by Fergus, Loarn, and Angus, three sons of a Dalriadic chieftain named Erc. Between them they consolidated the Irish conquests, both their own and those of the Riada people, into a territory more or less coterminous with the present county of Argyll. This latter name derives from the new Irish settlers: *Airer Gaedhil*, 'the coastal region of the Gaels.'

Of the sons of Erc, Angus, established himself in Islay. Loarn had his headquarters at Dunollie near Oban. After him is named that exquisitely scenic area of Scotland: The Firth of Loarn. Fergus, bet-ter known as *Fergus Mór*, Big Fergus, seems to have been head of the clan, and ruled as king of Dal Riada from the security of his hill-top stronghold at Dunadd, in Knapdale. Indeed, it may well have been Fergus himself who first established this citadel.

Within a century of the arrival of the sons of Erc, one of the royal line of Fergus Mór, Domingart by name, was declaring himself *Rí Alba* – King of Scotland. He came to an early grave because his claim to so grandiose a title was a mortal affront to those who

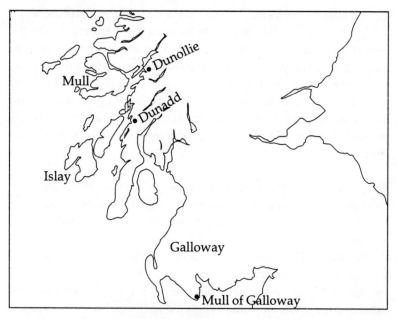

shared the country with him, and to none more than Brude Mac Maelchon, King of the Northern Picts, who saw to his destruction.

It was a showery July evening when I first climbed that historic outcrop of rock from which Domingart had gone to his grave. Despite the light mist and the lateness of the day, the view from the top was rewarding. Fergus had made a good choice. In time of peace he could gaze with pleasure over his flocks and herds on the plane below, while in time of war the same plane offered no cover for an approaching enemy.

Very little now remains of this Dalriadic capital, at least as far as human structures go. An archaeological notice at the site informs the visitor that Dunadd had 'a complex fortification, defended by four lines of walling on different levels'. As one ascends the terraces that walling system is sometimes barely traceable, at other times quite substantially evident. There are no traces of the many wooden dwelling houses that were enclosed by these stone ramparts. What are of great interest, however, are the rock-carvings close to the hilltop. Here, one may view some ogham script in an unknown language, together with the engraved outline of a boar, after the Pictish style of art. Nearby, cut into the solid rock, are a footprint and a basin. It is supposed that these were somehow connected with the rite of inauguration of kings, because Dunadd has long been considered to be the place where Dal Riada's monarchs were inaugurated. Apart from all that, Dunadd is an outstanding example of an early mediaeval fortification. It was a significant political centre for much of the time between about AD 500-1,000, and particularly around the year AD 500 it was outstanding for high quality metal work.

From the fifth to the seventh century, the Irish were not the only people on the move. Aside from earlier problems with the Romans, the Britons were now being pressed hard by Teutonic peoples crossing over the Straits of Dover from Denmark and the Netherlands. These included Angles, Saxons, Jutes, Mercians and others, who for literary convenience more than historical accuracy are generally termed *Anglo-Saxons* or simply *English*. Between the time of their arrival and the beginning of the eighth century, these Teutonic peoples had occupied virtually all of England and the lowlands of Scotland, but did not reach Ireland for over another thousand years – until King James VI of Scotland (I of England) planted their descendants in east Ulster.

At the same time as the Teutonic invasions, the Dal Riada influence in Pictland continued to expand and contract with the fortunes of war until, in the ninth-century, Pictish resistance finally faded and Kenneth Mac Alpine, King of Dal Riada, became king of all Scotland north of the Firth of Forth and the Firth of Clyde. In the two centuries following, Irish political, linguistic and cultural influence continued to expand south of the Forth and Clyde until, for a time, all of what we know today as Scotland was either wholly or partly Irish (Gaelic) speaking: Brittonic, Pictish and even Lowland Scots having adopted, for the most part, the language of their political masters.

CHAPTER 1

Galloway's White House

The first Christian century saw the gospel message penetrate Roman Britain. Archaeological research and unbroken tradition also testify to its existence in Dumfries and Galloway at an early period. Then, about the middle of the fourth century, there appeared the shadowy figure of Ninian. I say 'shadowy' because so much uncertainty surrounds him; it has even been suggested that the whole Ninian story is a construct! The Venerable Bede (d. 735), earliest historian of the English church and people, mentions him. St Aelred, the twelfth-century Cistercian abbot of Rievaulx in Yorkshire, wrote his life. According to Aelred, Ninian was the son of a Pictish chieftain in Galloway. He gives his date of birth as about AD 360, and says that he went to Rome and studied there in the reign of Pope Damasus (366-84). If so, Ninian was there in exciting times, for this was the age of Jerome, Ambrose and Augustine, Jerome being secretary to Pope St Damasus and a brilliant professor of scripture in the Christian capital. Under Pope St Siricius, the successor of Damasus, Ninian is said to have concluded his studies, been ordained bishop and sent back to his native land.

The return journey gave him the opportunity of visiting Marmoutier, one of the most renowned monasteries of the day and still under the leadership of St Martin of Tours. With the saint of Tours, Ninian must have discussed his plans and dreams, because, on his departure, Martin gave him an unusual present: a dozen monks who were skilled in the art of building.

Once he got back to the Kingdom of Strathclyde, Ninian found himself a suitable site on the Mull of Galloway, and, with the help of his skilled monks, built the first stone church ever seen in that part of the world. When the building was nearing completion, word came from the Continent that Martin had died at Tours, and Ninian, out of deference to his saintly benefactor, named the new church St Martin's. The local Britons, however, had another name for it. As they gazed on the new building and the whiteness of its walls, so different from their own wooden structures, they called it *Hwit-aern*, 'White House'. Hence, the latinised form *Candida Casa*, and modern Whithorn. With the passage of time, Ninian's foundation became a significant centre of learning, specifically in the fields of scripture and spirituality. Because of its reputation and size, it received yet another popular designation, that of *Magnum Monaster-ium*, 'The Great Monastery.'

It is difficult to trace with accuracy the extent of Ninian's mission-ary efforts. According to Bede, he was responsible for the conver-sion of the Southern Picts. This meant working not only in Galloway but north of the Firth of Forth and as far as the Grampians. But from church-dedications – more than sixty in number – it seems that his influence extended further. There is a chain of dedications running from Galloway through the midland valley and up the east coast as far as the Orkney Islands. And while working in Ullapool, I wondered if the name of Isle Martin in Loch Broom might not derive from the influence of *Candida Casa* or even its founder. Besides, as Daphne Pochin Mould observes, when Bede says that Ninian converted the southern Picts, in all probability he was work-ing from Ptolemy's map which puts Scotland lying on its back as it were, turning the east coast into a south coast, with its Pictish inhabitants appearing as 'Southern'.

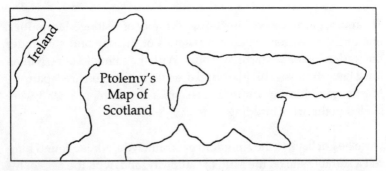

There is also a tradition in the Irish Midlands that Ninian worked there for a time and made a monastic foundation at Cloncurry in Co

Kildare. He is commemorated in a number of ancient Irish records, notably in the Festology (*Féilire*) of St Aengus of Tallaght.

Anybody vaguely familiar with the religious and disciplinary practices of early Celtic saints will readily understand why Ninian is presented as a man of austerity. It is said that during Lent he dined most frugally, and ate nothing at all from Holy Thursday evening until after celebrating the Holy Eucharist on Easter Morning. Like so many saints who came after him, Ninian found himself a retreat some distance away from his monastery where he could give himself to prayer and contemplation without interruption. His chosen spot, Ninian's Cave, is on the shore of Luce Bay, not far from Whithorn. After his death, in AD 432 according to tradition, his body was laid to rest in the monastic church which he and his community had built for the glory of God in the days of their youth.

The date AD 432 is also associated in tradition with St Patrick's arrival in Ireland. Within a generation or two of his coming, many young Irish aspirants to monastic life began to look to *Candida Casa* for inspiration and guidance. Among the first to make the journey to the Great Monastery was Enda, a young prince, who, on becoming a Christian, renounced his earthly kingdom of Oriel on the borders of Leinster and Ulster, preferring to take the boat across the North Channel to train as a monk. A flood of young Christian Ireland followed him: among them, we are told, Senan of Scattery, Fechin of Fore, Finian of Moville, Munchin of Limerick, Tighernach of Clones, Eoghan of Ardstraw, and Canice of Kilkenny. (And if the tradition be authentic, there also came over the waves to Scotland, one Thenog, a pagan girl who on more than one occasion was saved from death by calling on Mary the Mother of God, and who lived to become the mother of St Kentigern or *Mungo*, the founder and patron of Glasgow. Edana came too – that holy nun around whose tomb there grew up a burgh bearing her name, none other than Scotland's own capital city of Edinburgh.) Such was the reputation of *Candida Casa* as a school of spirituality that the Irish came in increasing numbers until eventually they built their own monastery, or at least had their own designated area.

All through the mediaeval period pilgrims flocked to Whithorn and
its adjacent Isle of Whithorn. Among the best known are Edward II
of England who came prior to being made king. He might fittingly
have come in penitential garb to make reparation for the sins of his
father, Edward I, whose savage behaviour earned him the sobri-
quet 'hammer of Scotland.' Instead, he came with a military force
and the Scots were so furious that they hid the statue of their
beloved saint. At Whithorn, king Robert the Bruce sought a cure in
the last stages of a wasting disease but died soon after. There his
son, David II, found healing from battle wounds. James III came on
pilgrimage as did his queen, Margaret of Denmark. And following
them there came James IV and James V.

Of all the Late Mediaeval pilgrims, James IV was probably the most
colourful. One of the greatest of Scottish kings, James was a man of
many talents and all-round goodness. He was the last Gaelic-speak-
ing king, a cultured man, with a capacity to appreciate, play, and
compose good music. Year by year, almost without interruption, he
walked from Stirling to Whithorn, not alone indeed, but like a true
Gaelic chieftain, with a lively following and plenty of music. Sadly,
his career was cut short in AD 1513 when, together with a great
number of the nobility and many bishops, he was slain on Flodden
Field. An ancient quatrain laments them thus:

I've heard them lilting at the ewes milking,
The flowers of the forest are a' wede away.
I ride single on my saddle,
For the flowers of the forest are a' wede away.

Another royal pilgrim to Whithorn, also with musical talent, came
in August 1563 – Mary Stuart, Queen of Scots, who 'had a voice
very sweet and good, for she sang very well, blending her voice
with the lute, which she touched so daintily with that fair white
hand.' (John Purser, in *Scotland's Music*, p 103, suggests that 'she
may even have composed the Galliards which bear her name, *The
Queen of Scots Galliard* and the *Galliarda la Royne d'Ecosse*, both courtly
dances, well-mannered, unpretentious, but lively'.) No doubt the
devout lady would have come again except for the troubles of the
time that led her first to prison, and later, on 8 February 1587, to the
executioner's block, where she met her death thanking God for the

grace to 'die for the honour of his name and of his church, catholic, apostolic and Roman.'

Among the immediate effects of the sixteenth-century Reformation on Whithorn were the suppression of the twelfth-century Prae-monstratentian Priory which had replaced the *Magnum Monast-erium*, and the proscribing of the pilgrimage. As in other centres of pilgrimage during the centuries of strife and persecution, people gathered to pray and celebrate on the Pattern Day (on or near the saint's or patron's feast) if the religious climate allowed. The first official post-Reformation pilgrimage was in 1924. Since then, such assemblies are a regular feature of Scottish Catholic life. In 1982, the Bishop of Rome, John Paul II, made the pilgrimage to *Candida Casa*, a fitting expression of gratitude and appreciation for the adventurous young man from Galloway who sixteen hundred years previously had gone on pilgrimage to Rome.

On a bright afternoon during a mission in Girvan, I borrowed the parish priest's car and drove down to Wigtonshire to visit the holy places associated with saint Ninian – the Isle of Whithorn, the Cave of St Ninian, and of course, Whithorn itself. In the latter, the keeper of the museum was enthusiastic about the holy places committed to his care. Excavations carried out there in the late twentieth century had revealed the footings of a little stone church. This was popularly acclaimed as the original *Candida Casa* built by Ninian and his companions in or about AD 397, but the scholars are doubtful. For the pilgrim, however, it is pleasing to sit quietly on those low walls which jut out from under the mediaeval priory church and know that one is close to, if not exactly on, the spot chosen by Ninian as 'the place of his resurrection.'

CHAPTER 2

'Iona of my Heart'

While my pilgrimage to Iona began from our monastery in Dundalk, I consider it to have really got underway at Queen Street railway station in Glasgow. The platform where I awaited the morning train to Oban was crowded with the daily commuters although it was not yet eight o'clock. When the incoming Edinburgh train came to a standstill it disgorged a chaotic scurrying mass of humanity, but in the midst of the chaos I discerned a loosely cohesive group with a substantial amount of luggage. Could they possibly be bound for Iona? I watched them re-group on the platform and ultimately board the Oban train. I followed at a distance and took my seat in the same carriage though at the opposite end. Shortly after, the '8.12-for-Oban' was on its way, due allowances having been made for Celtic time-keeping.

The question remained: were they going to Iona? They were certainly in holiday mood and their picnic supplies indicated that preparations had been made for a long journey. The focus of that happy little party was a beautifully featured gentle lady with a subdued but obvious charm, whom I later came to know as Mary Lauden. She was in the company of her husband, Bill, their children, and their neighbour, Joyce Cairns. Joyce was conspicuous by her dazzling white hair and artistic mien. Well, I thought, if these are going to be among my companions for a week on Iona, things are looking good.

The three-hour journey to Oban occasioned an uninterrupted feast of Highland scenery as the train sped northwards along the shores of the Clyde, Gare Loch and Loch Long to Tarbet and Loch Lomond. From Tarbet to Crianlarich, Ben Lomond on the far side of the lake and Ben More to the north of it dominated the skyline.

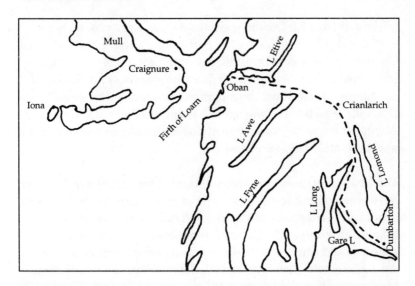

Then at Crianlarich the train took a westward route through Glen Lochy, past the southern entrance to Glen Orchy and on towards the Pass of Brander, leaving Loch Awe to our left and majestic Ben Cruachan to our right. The narrow Pass soon opened up to a panoramic view of romantic Loch Etive.

It is on the shores and hinterland of this lovely expanse of water that the folk tradition has set the most romantic portion of the tragic Celtic saga concerning the elopement of Deirdre of the Sorrows and Naoise son of Uisneach. Here, the two lovers are said to have survived on summer berries and winter mast together with the hunt of the hill and fish from the loch. The couple had eloped because King Conor McNessa of Ulster had planned to marry Deirdre who was said to have been the most beautiful woman in Ireland. But Deirdre wanted none other than Naoise, the handsome young warrior in the king's service. With false assurances of safety, the envoys of the king coaxed the lovers back home to Ireland where Naoise was promptly murdered. Deirdre, not willing to give herself to the king, jumped to her death from a speeding chariot.

The story of Deirdre and Naoise is not the only romantic tale associated with Loch Etive. At the Connel end of the loch we were able to catch a fleeting glimpse of Dunstaffnage castle where, in 1746, the celebrated Flora McDonald spent ten days as a prisoner on her way to trial and jail in London for her part in the escape of Bonnie Prince Charlie. And it was to Dunstaffnage at the dawn of history that the Irish brought a stone of great significance (probably not the *Lia Fáil*, or 'Stone of Destiny', but perhaps a coronation stone from Dunadd), which was removed to London and kept at Westminster Abbey for use in the coronation of English monarchs and which has now been returned to Scotland.

The Oban train came to a standstill right at the pier where the noon ferry was waiting to take its quota of passengers to Mull. By this time I had exchanged a few smiles and nods of recognition with the Edinburgh group. I had also surreptitiously glanced at their luggage tags and, sure enough, 'Iona' was clearly marked on each item. All I had to do then was to collect my ticket at the Caledonian MacBrayne office right there on the quayside and trail the Edinburgh pilgrims up the gangway of *The Island of Mull* without further care for travel arrangements.

If the scenes from the Glasgow-Oban train were beautiful, the loveliness that surrounded us for the forty minute crossing of the Firth of Loarn between Oban on the mainland and Craignure in Mull was truly intoxicating. Weather conditions were particularly favourable and wherever the eye fell in any direction, be it on sea or sky, distant mountains or shore-line hills, it fell on azure forms. Besides, we were never so far from land as to be denied some sight of historic and folkloric locations on the mainland and islands.

First, there was Oban's chief landmark, McCaig's Folly. It has dominated the town for a century. One may well wonder was it folly or grace, because McCaig, after whom the folly is named, was a generous and good man who spent his personal fortune in providing employment to alleviate the condition of his less fortunate townspeople. An Oban banker with family background in neighbouring Lismore, McCaig, in 1897, undertook the building of this magnificent granite rotunda modelled on the Colosseum in Rome. Money ran out during the construction phase and he never realised his dream of having within its walls an art gallery and museum.

Down at the shore, on the starboard side of the ferry, was another striking granite building: the Catholic cathedral of St Columba. Said by many experts to be the finest modern Gothic building in all of Britain, it measures no more than a hundred and fifty feet in length and is fronted by a ninety-foot tower. The architect, Sir Gilbert Scott, chose pink granite from Peterhead and artistically set it off against blue granite from Inverawe. The roof is of magnificent Kentish oak beams and the yellow and brown tints in the slate blend in with the stone work. The overall result is a building of beauty, simplicity and elegance.

Rising up behind the cathedral was the green hill of Dunollie, the ancient capital from which Loarn, son of Erc, and his descendants ruled. A short distance beyond the cathedral and on the right of the road that winds by the sea is 'The Dog Stone.' It is a huge natural pillar of granite which folk tradition identifies as the very stone where Fionn MacCool, the semi-mythical Celtic hero, used to tie up his dog, Bran. Next, a little higher on the slopes of the wooded hill are the ruins of a castle which for centuries was the court of the MacDoughals, Lords of Loarn. No sooner has the ferry passed the MacDoughal stronghold than a long green and almost treeless island comes into view. This is the illustrious Lismore of St Moluag which boasted the cathedral church of Argyll and the Isles in pre-Reformation times. On the port side is the sheltering Island of Kerrera, and thereafter the coast of Mull with the thirteenth-century Dewart Castle of the MacLeans as its most prominent feature.

We disembarked at Craignure, ('the cliff of the yews'), on the Island of Mull. A fleet of buses was at the service of passengers to take them to their various destinations. Most were taking the 38-mile journey through Glenmore, down the Ross of Mull to Fionnphort and Iona. Mull is a large, beautiful island with more than three hundred miles of coastline. Not least among its attractions are its lakes, mountains, cliffs, ocean scenery, stone circles, standing stones, cairns and crannogs, together with its many thousands of deer and the eagles that make their home around the 3,171-foot Ben Mór, the island's highest mountain.

Iona is not the only off-shore island of Mull. It has many, notably

Ulva and Erraid. Robert Louis Stevenson, the author of *Kidnapped* was a native of Mull. Memories of Glenmore and the Lussa river inform his writings, and Erraid is the prototype of his *Treasure Island*. The ancestors of David Livingstone, the explorer, came from Ulva, as did General Lachlan MacQuarry, 'the Father of Australia,' who died in 1824. 'Ulva's Isle' also is the inspiration for Thomas Campbell's poem *Lord Ullin's Daughter*.

It was somewhere on the far side of Bunessan village, in the Ross of Mull, that I caught my first glimpse of Iona. This was the *'mons gaudi'* (the hill of rejoicing) so longed for by mediaeval pilgrims. From there I could see the gleaming white sands of Iona and my heart beat faster. The last leg of the journey was the seven-minute ferry trip from Fionnphort across the Sound of Iona to St Ronan's Bay. Ahead of us was Martyr's Bay on the port side, Dún Í (the highest point on the island) on starboard, and between both, on the site of Columcille's original foundation, stood the restored thirteenth-century Benedictine abbey.

But before we go ashore, as it were, the question must be asked: Who was this Colmcille (or *Columba*, his preferred name in Scotland), whose life touched Iona and raised it from the anonymity of a hundred Scottish islands to become a light to the world? In the course of my work in Scotland, I have noticed that St Colmcille's life prior to his arrival on Iona is scarcely known there at all. This is unfortunate for at least two reasons: firstly, because the man had more than half his life lived out before leaving Ireland, and secondly, by comparison with virtually all other Celtic saints, there is a fund of information from which we may derive some answers, notably, the writings of St Adamnán in the seventh century, St Bede in the eighth, an anonymous biographer in the twelfth, and a sixteenth-century *Life* by Manus O'Donnell. Their subject was indeed a legend in his own lifetime and succeeding generations have likewise been fascinated by this extraordinary prince, priest, prophet, poet, monk, abbot, scribe, scholar, diplomat and saint.

Colmcille was born at Gartan, Co Donegal, in Ireland. The traditional date of his birth is 7 December, AD 521. Although he was eligible for the high kingship of Ireland, he turned his back on any such ambitions in favour of the monastic life. We are told that Colmcille pursued native lore and learning at the feet of Gemman (described as a Leinsterman and a Christian bard), studied spirituality at St Enda's monastery on the Aran islands, and pursued his theological studies in Co Meath under St Finian of Clonard – 'The Teacher of the saints of Ireland'. It is said that he was ordained deacon by St Finian of Moville in Co Down, and raised to the priesthood by St Etchen, at Clonfad in Co Westmeath, just a few miles from Kinnegad. It is estimated that he must have been about thirty years of age at the time.

According to St Aengus of Tallaght, Colmcille, together with three friends, Comgall, Ciarán and Cainnech (Canice), set out for St Mobhi's monastery at Glasnevin on the banks of the river Tolka in Dublin. Their stay was short-lived because Mobhi temporarily disbanded the community in view of the impending *Búidhe Chonnaill* or Yellow Plague, so called because the skins of its victims turned yellow. Colmcille then returned to Derry on the banks of the Foyle. The site of his monastery there is identified as that occupied by St Columba's (Long Tower) church, and the city itself is inseparable from his name and memory, *Doire Cholmcille*, Derry of Colmcille. An ancient Irish poem attributed to the saint himself, but in fact of a later date, proclaims:

> Why I love Derry is this:
> for its purity, for its brightness;
> for its absolute fulness of white angels
> from one end to the other.

From Derry began the round of monastic foundations attributed to him. Durrow in Co Offaly is the most authentic in terms of being founded by the man himself. Kells is the most famous, though there is a shade of doubt as to whether he was the actual founder. Tradition is generous in ascribing foundations to him and one writer credits him with three hundred, an exaggeration surely but a point well made:

> Three hundred he measured, without fault,
> Of churches fair, 'tis true;
> And three hundred splendid, lasting books

Noble-bright he wrote.

An aura of uncertainty surrounds the motive for Colmcille's departure from Ireland in AD 563. St Adamnán, his biographer and ninth
successor as Abbot of Iona, says that he left 'because he wished to
become a pilgrim for Christ's sake'. Over against this straightfor-
ward and exalted motive, there is a later tradition to the effect that
the saint's departure was due to a row with a friend and a row with
the High King which culminated in the battle of Cúl Dreimne. This
latter tradition has no basis in the earliest and most authentic
records. Whether it has a basis at all is questionable. It is more likely
to have been a romantic tale.

Romance or otherwise the story is this: St Finian of Moville, while
on a visit to Rome, acquired a copy of the best and most up-to-date
translation of the psalms which St Jerome had made from the original languages. Colmcille saw it, liked it, and secretly copied it by
night. On discovering this act of piracy by his erstwhile pupil,
Finian was angry and demanded the immediate return of the copy.
Colmcille refused. Finian took his case to the High King, Diarmuid
O'Carroll. The latter handed down what is considered to be the first
recorded decision on copyright material, which was: 'To every cow
its calf and to every book its copy.' Colmcille was unrepentant to
the point of involving himself and his kinsmen, the Northern Uí
Néill, in a battle with the High King's forces. The engagement took
place at Cúl Dreimne on the slopes of Benbulben, within sight of
one of Colmcille's early foundations at Drumcliffe, Co Sligo. The
battle, fought in AD 561, was a victory for the northern Uí Néill, but
Colmcille's confessor imposed a penance on him to the effect that
he should go into exile and win as many souls for Christ as had
been lost in the battle. Furthermore, he should never more set eyes
on Ireland nor set foot on her soil. That's the story – romantic
indeed! The trouble with it is that neither Adamnán – the saint's
seventh-century biographer – nor Bede, nor the old Irish *Life* make
any reference to it.

But the aura of uncertainty won't go away for another reason. In the
library of the Royal Irish Academy in Dublin, there is a manuscript
of great antiquity which tradition claims to be the actual copy of the
psalms which Colmcille made in the year AD 560. It is known as the

Cathach (Battle reliquary) from the fact that in mediaeval times it was carried in battle as a sort of talisman by the O'Donnells of Donegal, who were Colmcille's own people and a sept of the above-mentioned Uí Néill. Archaeologists recognise the manuscript to be old, as old perhaps as the late sixth or early seventh-century. They are further agreed that the manuscript was written by one person and that it was written in a hurry. Is it Colmcille's copy? The answer may be found as likely in the heart as in the head.

At the age of forty-two, then, Colmcille in the company of twelve monks, symbolic of Jesus and the twelve, set sail from Ireland as Adamnán says, 'because he wished to become a pilgrim for Christ's sake'. St Bede, writing about AD 721, confirms Adamnán's statement thus: 'There came from Ireland into Britain a famous priest and abbot, a monk by habit and life, whose name was Columba, to preach the Word of God.' Prior to his departure, he had already accomplished in Ireland more than several energetic people might have done in their combined lifetimes. His going must have been a source of sorrow to many for he was not only a holy man, but, according to the *'Lives,'* he was tall and handsome; affable, too, despite a seemingly unjustified reputation for quick temper; a poet of high accomplishment, born to rule, with the sweetness and power of his voice said to have been verging on the miraculous. The impact of his exile on the Irish psyche came home to me strongly as recently as 1995. During a mission in Granard, Co Longford, I took holy communion to the late saintly Maeve Brady ('Queenie') and afterwards spoke to her of Columcille and his departure from Ireland. Anybody not knowing that the man of whom she spoke lived in the sixth-century would readily be forgiven for thinking that he had only left her fireside and his own native land the previous week, such was the warmth and immediacy of her sentiments.

Scotland of that time was a complex place, with its Northern Picts, Southern Picts, Galloway Picts, Britons of Strathclyde, Scots of Dal Riada, and the latest arrivals, the Teutonic Angles and Lothians. Immediately prior to Colmcille's arrival, the Dalriadic Scots were at an all-time low, having suffered a heavy defeat at the hands of Brude Mac Maelchon. In fact, some scholars are of the opinion that this might be one of the reasons for his coming among them, since

they were his own people and spoke his own Gaelic language.
According to tradition, when Colmcille sailed from Derry he made
first landfall at the Inner Hebridean island of Islay. That tradition
still lives in Islay and the people are proud of it, as I quickly discovered when working there in 1993. The romantic account of his exile
has him put to sea once more because Islay is still within sight of
Ireland. The next recorded landfall is at *Port 'a Curaich* (the Harbour
of the Curragh or Coracle) at the south end of the Isle of Iona. It was
Pentecost Sunday, May 12 AD 563. Again, the romantic account has
him immediately climbing *Cairn Cúl rí Éirin* to satisfy himself that
Ireland was out of sight; and hence the name *'The Cairn of one's back
to Ireland.'*

It was obvious from the outset that Iona was no Garden of Eden.
Measuring three and a half miles in length and about half that in
width, much of its surface is hill and moor. Its western shore,
exposed as it is to the full force of Atlantic storms, and its rocky
coastline and treacherous currents, offered little by way of easy
access. Nevertheless, fish and seals were plentiful while the tiny
western coastal plain (the *Machair*), together with flat and fertile
land in the sheltered east, offered the possibility of wresting a simple livelihood from land and sea. Colmcille chose a spot in the fairly
level and sheltered eastern part of the island as the site for his
monastery. Here the newcomers built a wooden church, together
with monastic cells and domestic buildings, and probably enclosed
the lot within a wooden palisade. With the passage of time the
enclosure fence was upgraded to a solid earthen rampart, parts of
which still exist and most of which is traceable in outline.

Both from a missionary and political viewpoint, the choice of Iona
was a judicious one. Although it had Neolithic and Iron Age inhabitants, it seems to have been uninhabited at the time of Colmcille's
arrival. Politically, it was on the border between Dal Riada and
Pictland, and there is some evidence to suggest that the founder
exercised a delicate diplomacy by getting permission to occupy the
island both from the vanquished ruler of Dal Riada and the victori-
ous Brude Mac Maelchon.

Dealing with the Dal Riada folk was simple enough. After all, they were of his own kin and creed. It was quite otherwise with the Picts. In or about AD 565, Colmcille went to Inverness to speak to Brude. His mission failed. He tried again, proceeding once more through the Great Glen, travelling the full length of Loch Ness and its river until he found himself before the fortress of the potentate. But this time he was accompanied by his friends Comgall and Cainneach (Canice), both of whom were Irish Picts and conversant with the language of King Brude. This second mission was a resounding success because, it seems, Brude not only confirmed him in his possession of Iona but also gave him permission to work in Pictland.

All this opened the way for Columba's missionaries to bring the Christian message where it had not yet been preached, or to fan the flame again where it had grown cold in the centuries after Ninian's death. Nobody knows for sure the extent of the Columban mission and some recent scholarly works would have us minimise it. What we do know, however, is that the mainland of Scotland, as well as the Orkney Islands, the Inner and Outer Hebrides, and elsewhere are dotted with the remains of Columban dedications.

For the thirty-five years of his life on Iona, Columba led his monks in prayer, study and apostolic endeavour. They risked life and limb for the sake of the gospel. Using the natural waterways of loch and sea, they journeyed far and wide, and when waterways ran out, they placed their upturned curraghs on their sturdy shoulders and continued through primeval forests, or over rough moor and steep mountains. The history and topography of Scotland was never the same after these soldiers of Christ had passed.

Remote as Iona is, St Colmcille, like so many of his sainted contemporaries, found it necessary to find a quiet place for prayer. The particular spot chosen by him is described by Adamnán as being 'in the woods' about half a mile distant from the monastery. The footings of a stone cell at a spot fitting the description is thought to be Colmcille's place of retreat.

While attending to prayer and contemplation, Columcille did not shun involvement in civic and political affairs. At Iona in AD 574,

he crowned Aidan King of Dal Riada, the first such Christian ceremony in Britain. After his second visit to Inverness there is no further talk of war between Brude Mac Maelchon and the Irish of Dal
Riada. The saint, according to Adamnán's account, was back and
forth to Ireland at least ten times. At the convention of Drumceat
near Limavady in Co Derry in AD 575, he was accompanied by King
Aidan and secured for him the political, military and financial independence of Scottish Dal Riada. There too, he successfully pleaded
on behalf of the bards who had become so powerful and overbear-
ing that their suppression was imminent. Colmcille's middle-
ground diplomacy carried the day, and the poets, musicians and
historians of Ireland never forgot it of him.

In all Columban monasteries there was a regime of prayer and
manual labour. The Eucharist was celebrated on Sundays and holy
days. Saturday was a day of rest in preparation for the Sunday
liturgy, seen as the chief work of the week. Priest members concelebrated the Eucharistic Service (*Mass*). If a bishop was present, he
was accorded pride of place and, as a special mark of respect for
him, nobody concelebrated. Holy communion was not taken very
frequently but, when it was, it was generally under both kinds. All
communicated at Easter.

Manual labour was not an optional extra, nor was it a devised penitential exercise. It was a necessary element for sustaining human
life on the island. The Columban monks kept cattle, sheep and horses.
The milk and milk-products from the cattle and sheep were important to monastic diet, while the wool from the sheep provided the
raw material for the monks' clothing. The seas could be relied upon
for an adequate supply of fish, but due to the uncertainty of Iona
weather, provision of grain and vegetables was more problematic.
A farm in Tiree run by a sub-community was the chief source of
Iona's grain supply. On the home-front, the Machair (Gaelic: *mágh*,
a plain) by the western sea was much cultivated.

For myself, one of the most moving experiences in Iona is to stand
on a patch of high ground overlooking the Machair and contemplate the ridge-traces of mediaeval cultivation where so many
saints sweated and laboured. This surely is holy ground if ever the

term deserves to be applied outside of its biblical context. Here at the water's edge Colmcille spent many a day wresting a living from the soil and, besides the anonymous multitude of holy people who came with him and after him, we can name St Báithín, St Adamnán, St Ernan, St Oran, the two St Suibhnes, St Blaithmaic, St Euchadius, St Conan, St Finan, St Colman, St Cuchuivne, St Egbert, St Cormac, St Killen, St Dorstan, St Laisren, St Kenneth (Canice), St Crunmael, St Aidan of Lindisfarne and his good friend St Oswald the king. Added to these are the numerous sainted monks who visited Colmcille and his successors on the island and who, no doubt, pitched in their lot with the monastic work-force during the busy days of spring and harvest.

St Oran, one of the original twelve companions who sailed with Colmcille, was the first to die on the island. The monastic burial ground, *Reilig Odhráin,* was named after him. The founder himself was probably buried outside the church door and a little to the right. A small chapel now marks the spot. Báithín, his immediate successor, was buried where St Oran's chapel now stands. With the passage of time the fame of Iona was such that the royalty brought their dead for burial there, and it is said that sixty kings – forty-eight Scottish, four Irish and eight Norwegian – rest in St Oran's Graveyard, among them MacBeth and Duncan of Shakespearean fame:

Ross: Where is Duncan buried?

McDuff: Carried to Colm-kill
The sacred storehouse of his predecessors
And guardian of their bones.

It is evident from Adamnán's *Life of Colmcille,* that living on Iona was rarely less than a struggle. The food-chain was never too secure and one or two bad seasons could reduce the community's resources to danger point. Adamnán speaks of the joy of Colmcille shortly before death when he noted that the granary had enough to see the community through the year ahead.

Shortly before his death, on June 9, AD 597, the holy founder made his *turas bháis,* his *death journey.* Visiting every place on the island, he blessed the farms and the crops, the livestock and the barns. He paused for rest on the return journey to the monastery, and if he

did, the old white horse came shedding tears of sadness at what it
knew to be their final meeting, for animals have a keen sense of
things beyond the capacity of most humans. Back in his cell, the
abbot took up his accustomed transcription of the bible; and having
written the line from Psalm 34: 'But they that seek the Lord shall
lack no good thing,' he laid down his pen for the last time and said:
'Let Báithín write what follows.' His final words of advice to the
brethren were from the core of the gospel: an exhortation to live in
peace and love. Hurrying to the church for the midnight Office, he
collapsed on the sanctuary. Though unable to speak, he managed
with brother Diarmuid's assistance to raise his hand in a final bene-
diction over the community. And so he died.

During these last moments, a great light surrounded the church.
From time to time, I have heard lecturers casually dismiss the reference to this phenomenon as pious mediaeval fiction. But para-nor-
mal phenomena are part of Hebridean life-experience, not only in
the sixth century but in the twentieth as well. From my own mission
work in the Hebrides I have often met people who still experience
such phenomena as 'the ball of light'– associated with death or
birth – as well as experiences where the past or future invades the
present. In the Hebrides, there seems to be but a very thin line
between 'our' reality and other realities. Conscious of this same thin
line, the Presbyterian patriarchal figure, George MacLeod, who fell
in love with Iona and restored the mediaeval Benedictine abbey
there, was fond of quoting Francis Thompson's *The Kingdom of God*:

> The angels keep their ancient places –
> Turn but a stone, and start a wing!
> 'Tis ye, 'tis your estranged faces,
> That miss the many-splendoured thing.

After Colmcille's death, the monastery flourished for two centuries.
Then, because of the Viking terror, monastic life became virtually
unsustainable on the island. Raids are recorded for AD 795, 802,
806, 825, 976, 986. For this reason, at the beginning of the ninth century, the entire Columban administration moved to Kells in the
Irish Midlands. With the decline in Celtic monasticism in the twelfth
century, the remaining monks in Iona were ousted in favour of a
community of Benedictines from Durham. These were the builders

of the fine stone abbey and the nearby convent for the Canonesses of St Augustine. Despite the official passing of the Celtic community, it is probable that some of the remaining Irish monks were accepted into the new community. Certainly, there is an Irish architectural stamp on much of the stonework in both buildings. For a long time the community of religious women was predominantly Irish, albeit under the rule of Norse superiors. The ruins of the convent are among the finest that remain in Scotland and, in time, who knows but another George-MacLeod may restore them.

During the late mediaeval period, prior to the Reformation, life went on as in most other monastic communities, except that on Iona conditions continued to be grim. The archaeological excavations of what is thought to have been the nuns' graveyard reveals that this was the burial place of a large number of people, mostly women, none of whom had children, none of whom had died violently, and none of whom had lived beyond about the age of forty.

From its devastation during the sixteenth-century Reformation down to George MacLeod's restoration in the twentieth, the monastery on Iona lay in ruins.

Did Colmcille foresee it all? A prophesy attributed to him, says that he did:

> In Iona of my heart, Iona of my love, where monks' voices were, shall be lowing of cattle. But ere the world shall come to an end, Iona will be as it was.

For the Catholic community at least, Iona is not yet 'as it was.' But there are signs of movement in that direction. At *Cnoc a Chalmain* a new Catholic house of prayer with a small chapel is being officially opened this year, the 1400th anniversary of the saint's death, while the ecumenical *Iona Community* is in existence for more than half a century. In a sermon at Iona, Cardinal Winning of Glasgow said: 'The path to further reconciliation… cannot lie in brooding over our wounds, or in mutual recriminations, but in a continual series of creative experiments born of good will.' Iona today is conducting such an experiment and it was to participate in it, for a week at any rate, that I stepped ashore.

Most Celtic holy places in Scotland and elsewhere are, nowadays, little more than archaeological sites. Iona is different. Under God, the Very Rev George MacLeod (1895-1991), is primarily responsible for changing the fortunes of this 'holy of holies' in the Celtic world. Govan, the area of Glasgow where he ministered in the 1930s, had high unemployment. George hadn't money to assist his people but if it was work they wanted then he had no shortage of it, because he was determined to restore the ruined thirteenth-century Benedictine abbey on the Isle of Iona in the Inner Hebrides. And so, shortly before the outbreak of World War II, he and his band of unemployed volunteers set out on what must have been seen at the time as one of the craziest undertakings imaginable.

On Iona, having provided themselves with temporary accommodation and whatever essential facilities were required, they set to work. While establishing an adequate food-chain for his team, George, being a man of God, ensured that the spiritual food-chain was also in order. Day by day, as well as taking off his coat to shovel and pick, he prayed for some considerable time with his closest associates. Observing this, his volunteer force inquired if they, too, might be allowed to share prayer with him; and so there came into being the Iona Community and the main structures of their daily life. Ever since, at a certain time in the morning and in the late evening, the entire staff repairs to the abbey church for prayer.

The workers donated their labours. Would others perhaps donate the necessary money and materials for the restoration? George wrote letters, begged and cajoled; and as in the gospel story, if people didn't give from the sheer generosity of their hearts, they gave to get peace from George. Not only individuals were approached but companies and governments. The most spectacular response was from the Norwegians, who sent a ship-load of timber in reparation for the destruction wrought on Iona by their Viking ancestors over a thousand years previously. If you ever happen to be in the abbey dining room, observe the ceiling and roof and see for yourself what a fine act of reparation it was!

Work for youth was very much in the mind and heart of MacLeod. Side by side with the restoration of the abbey, which continued from 1938-67, he ran summer camps, accommodating the young people in old wooden cabins. In the late 1960s, when work on the abbey was nearing completion, and the wooden cabins were deteriorating by the year, he turned his thoughts to the idea of a purpose-built centre which would cater for youth, for families and for the disabled. It would also be a centre for international reconciliation. Today it stands, relatively unobtrusive on the Iona landscape, and named appropriately *The MacLeod Centre*.

About three miles from the abbey, on the Ross of Mull, at a spot called Camas (Gaelic for a *small bay* or *cove*), the Iona Community manages another property devoted to the service of youth. The buildings there were originally constructed as a salmon fishing station owned by the Duke of Argyll. The duke leased them to MacLeod at a nominal rent. In the course of time, this venue has become more and more a centre for delinquent youngsters from Borstals. Here, in a beautiful setting, the young people have an opportunity of experiencing outdoor activities on land and sea, as well as engaging in discussion, and worship too, if they so wish. For many youngsters, the holiday in Camas is the moment of grace that has changed their lives.

The pilgrimage to Iona has also been a source of grace for myself. During my stay in 1992, I became friendly with the then wardens, Philip and Alison Newell, who invited me back to lecture on Celtic spirituality. This offer I gladly accepted, and through it I have made a lot of friends across the religious divide, thus in a small way realising some of the hopes of George MacLeod. Unfortunately, I never had the pleasure of meeting the man himself as he passed away some weeks before I became involved with the community. During my stay I learned that the Joyce Cairns whom I had first seen on the Oban train had done the last sketch of the nonagenarian MacLeod, a work later purchased by the National Gallery in Edinburgh.

Pilgrims who book into the abbey are not just paying guests; they are part of the establishment for the duration of their stay; in a sense they become 'the Iona community.' They are assigned various chores relating to house maintenance as well as participating actively in the morning and evening church services. Every

Wednesday a designated person from the Iona Community is deputed to lead a pilgrimage to the holy places of the Island, starting at the 8th-century St Martin's Cross, and including the Convent (Nunnery), the Hill of the Angels, the Machair, *Port a' Churraic* (Columba's Bay), the Hermit's Cell, Dún Í, and St Oran's Chapel where the final prayer is recited.

As well as being a religious exercise the Wednesday pilgrimage is a community-builder. It is relaxed and rural, with plenty of fresh air, beautiful scenery and a welcome picnic lunch on the Machair about half way through. At the end of the four or five hour outing, one can always enjoy a swim in the clear blue waters that surround Iona, or join a friend in the pleasant atmosphere of the coffee shop which is a small unobtrusive *refugium peccatorum* which would surely meet with the whole-hearted approval of St Columcille.

On a personal note, the highlight of my own pilgrimage was having my feet washed at the end of the journey. It wasn't simply the fact that the kind act was performed by Jean Matthews, a Southern Baptist from the U.S.A., nor indeed the gospel symbolism of the gesture, but the foundation of that symbol: the sheer luxury of having one's feet washed after walking without shoes for several hours.

CHAPTER 3

'Lios Mór in Alba'

'Lios Mór in Alba' is the term used in the *Martyrology of Donegal* and other ancient Irish chronicles to distinguish the island of Lismore in Scotland from Lismore-Mochuda in Waterford, Ireland. For long I had an ambition to visit that island since it was here in the shelter of a low ridge that St Moluag made his monastic foundation. Tradition assigns the event to AD 562. It was not until the summer of 1995 that a suitable opportunity arose for the realisation of my ambition. I had a weekend break between two retreats which I was conducting in Craig Lodge, Dalmally, in the West Highlands. Though the weather wasn't very promising, I betook myself to Oban and there boarded a vessel bound for the island of Lismore in Loch Linnhe in the Firth of Loarn, a journey of some fifty minutes. The afternoon was wet as we sailed out from Oban pier.

The Caledonian MacBrayne ferry was relatively small – Lismore has only about 160 inhabitants and it is not on the regular tourist trail as are the neighbouring islands of Mull and Iona. On this particular Friday, however, the little lounge was crammed with exuberant youngsters together with their more sedate teachers and elders, and some visitors. A lovely silver cup was being shown off and passed around. A woman sitting beside me, Doranne Willis, read the curiosity in my face and eyes. 'They won a junior bilingual cabaret competition at the Mod in Oban today,' she said. This ice-breaking sentence led to further conversation. Doranne is a retired teacher. 'It is my first visit to Lismore,' said I. 'Have you booked accommodation?' I hadn't. 'It will be particularly difficult to find a place to stay,' she continued, 'as there is a big crowd on the island for the weekend. Are you going to the *céilídh*?' On realising my total ignorance of life on Lismore, she informed me that there was a *céilídh* that very night in the island hall. A wedding had taken place

in England some time previously and, since the bride had roots in
Lismore, she and her husband had come to the island to celebrate
the event among her own people.

Wondering if I might have to spend the night under the open sky, I
drew the conversation back to the question of finding digs. Yes,
Doranne was virtually certain that Lismore's limited tourist accommodation was completely booked up, and then added with an air of
supreme confidence, 'Fiona will look after you.' Her gaze switched
to a strikingly lovely young woman who sat across from us with
eyes closed in an attempt to get a few moments rest after an obvi-
ously demanding day. At the sound of her name, Fiona's large
intelligent eyes opened inquiringly. 'This gentleman needs accommodation,' said Doranne who, from her school experience was used
to handling people and their problems, 'will you be able to find him
a place or keep him in your own home?' Without discussion or
question, the young woman gently indicated that she would see to
my welfare. At this point the ferry was docking at Achnacrois (the
Field of the Cross). The invitation to the *céilídh* which had already
been issued to me in the course of our conversation was now
renewed with even greater enthusiasm, and as we parted I assured
her that I'd be there. I was already at home in Lismore before setting
foot on it.

On the pier I asked Fiona for instructions as to how I might get to
her house and what was the cost of B&B. She told me that she did
not do B&B at all but hastened to add that I'd have lodgings for the
night and welcome. I apologised for intruding but she dismissed
that as being 'no bother'. She gave me directions to her house and
with that I abandoned my ruck-sack into the back of the pick-up
truck which was taking her and some others to their respective destinations. Winding my way up the hill from the pier I gave a helping hand to a girl who was pushing a bike heavily laden with goods
from the mainland. We exchanged some words and greetings in
Gaelic, for that is a living language in Lismore. Presently she said,
'*Seo é mo thig*' (this is my home), and we parted.

Here I was, then, a lone pilgrim on the long green island of Lismore;
a dream of thirty years had come true. The rain had cleared, the sun

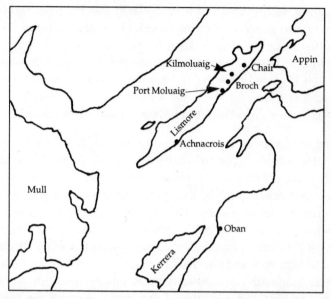

was shining, it was ten minutes to six on an evening in early summer, and the many-voiced birds were singing aloud what I was singing silently in my heart – praise and thanks to God for this day and this place. The surrounding hills of Loarn and the islands were beautiful.

So this was the island chosen by St Moluag as 'the place of his resurrection'. As with so many early Irish saints, details of his life are skimpy and uncertain. He is said to have been an Irish Pict, first a disciple of St Brendan the Navigator, and later schooled in the monastic life at St Comgall's monastery at Bangor in Co Down. Moluag's missionary work was spectacular and perhaps on a par with that of his contemporary on Iona. Despite the fact that he had no Adamnán to chronicle his illustrious career as had Colmcille, his name and fame have survived in the living folk tradition of his spiritual children in the green island of Lismore in Alba.

On the ferry from Oban somebody had told me the macabre tale of the race between Colmcille and Moluag. It is said that these two wonderful saints were rivals for possession of the island. As their curraghs approached the land, Colmcille was inching ahead of his rival, but the resourceful Moluag chopped off his own thumb and, flinging it ashore ahead of him, declared that his flesh and blood were first in possession of the island. (This story is taken straight from the pagan folklore relating to the eponymous founder of the province of Ulster except that in the original story it was an arm that was chopped off – the 'red hand of Ulster'!) It need hardly be added that Colmcille – who for some reason gets a very bad press on occasions such as this – lost his temper and cursed the place.

Along the roadway I paused often to contemplate the scenery and enjoy the sunshine. The air was light and fresh. A grey heron laboriously lifted off its rocky perch as I came over the brow of a hill. Cattle momentarily raised their large curious eyes in my direction and then resumed grazing. The larks accompanied my every step with joyful song. At the road junction where I had been directed to take a right turn, I paused to examine a young oak which had managed to take root and survive on the face of a little cliff. Beside it, and clinging with equal tenacity to the inhospitable cliff, were two purple orchids and a scatter of primroses. Around the turn the number and variety of wild flowers increased: bluebells and buttercups, water lilies galore, wild garlic in full bloom. And larks, larks, larks everywhere.

My rucksack came into view at a doorway. Fiona's surely? Indeed it was. In I went cheerily but my cheerfulness became forced and artificial as I tried to be free and easy in an atmosphere that was palpably tense and uncertain. Fiona introduced me to her husband Colin and their children, Rachel and Christopher. Realising that something was amiss I more or less apologised for my existence – certainly for my existence in that house at that moment – and assured Fiona that I'd find alternative accommodation. She said that she'd find me a suitable place and with that I left the house and continued on my pilgrimage, puzzled but not really upset, for the whole purpose of my going to Lismore was to be a pilgrim.

Fiona had provided me with a map of the Island. It was invaluable. Now the site of St Moluag's sixth-century monastic foundation, as well as the remains of the mediaeval Catholic cathedral, together with the hollowed rock known as *Moluag's Chair* were all identifiable. Equally important, they were measurable in terms of walking distance. At seven o'clock in the evening I arrived at Kilmoluaig, the spot where St Moluag had founded his monastery. From here he had gone far and wide by land and sea, spreading the gospel in the Hebrides, up the Great Glen, and as far as 'Tyle,' which is variously interpreted to be the Orkneys, or the Shetlands, or even Iceland. Places dedicated to his memory are numerous but not always readily recognisable – among them, Moluoc, Mortlach, Malloch, Kilmolowoc. (The variety stems largely from the expansion of his original name which is '*Lú*'. With the honorific' '*mo*' it becomes '*Molúa*'; while the endearing suffix – '*oc*', '*ag*', or '*aig*' – makes it *Moluoc*, *Moluag*, or *Moluaig*, literally, 'My little Lú.) Nor are the annals stinting in their praise of this bishop and abbot who founded a hundred churches (i.e. a large number) and dedicated so many of them to Mary, the Mother of God.

Aside from Lismore, his chief foundations were at Mortlach in Banffshire and Rosemarkie in Ross-shire. That Moluag lived to extreme old age seems certain, but no such certainty exists in relation to where he died and where he was first buried. June 25 is generally accepted as the day of his passing and AD 592 as the year. Although he was probably buried at Rosemarkie, his remains were later translated to his chief foundation at Kilmoluaig in Lismore and venerated there for centuries. Tradition points to Port Moluaig in Lismore as the saint's first landing place. It also points to it as the spot where his relics were brought ashore when being translated from Rosemarkie. Close by, there is a fresh water spring known as *Tobar na Sláinte* (the well of health) and said to be possessed of healing properties. It was a place of pilgrimage until the middle of the nineteenth century.

The church at the monastic settlement of Kilmoluaig was of such importance that, some time prior to AD 1189, it became the cathedral for the diocese of Argyll and was dedicated to its founder. But the cathedral church which was burned to the ground at the Reformation does not seem to have been older than the fourteenth century. After the Reformation, the remains of the building was used as a place of worship, sometimes by Anglicans, at other times by Presbyterians, and at yet other times allowed to remain untended so that Catholics used the interior as a burial ground. Then, in 1749, the Presbyterian community re-roofed the old choir which has ever since served as their parish church of Lismore.

In 1814, workmen near Kilmichael, Glassary, not far from Dunadd, found a bronze bell-shrine of twelfth-century date. The iron bell inside was from the seventh century, and is thought to be the one which, according to the *Aberdeen Breviary*, Moluaig had cast for use in his monastery in Lismore. Both bell and shrine are now preserved in the National Museum of Antiquities in Edinburgh.

Here I was, then, less than two hours after my arrival on the island, at the goal of my pilgrimage. Entering the empty church, I went on my knees and kissed the holy ground before spending some time in prayer. Then I examined the interior of the building. The sedilia and piscina together with some carved-head ornamentation were preserved *in situ* since the high middle ages. The church would seem to have been refurbished in the not too distant past. No longer did the pulpit dominate the sanctuary. There was a measure of equality of status between it and the communion table – an indication of theological developments reflected in the architecture of many Presbyterian churches in Scotland.

Outside were the footings of several cells from the early Christian period. Clearly discernible, too, was the outline of a relatively large building which probably dated from the same era and measured 45x30 feet. I wondered if this could have been a chapel. The scale of 1.5:1 measurements were certainly typical of early Irish church buildings, but the overall measurements seemed to be on the large side. At any rate, I walked around it clockwise reciting the *Pater Noster*, for it is my custom on such occasions as this to pray the Lord's Prayer in Latin in union with all the holy people who did so in times past and who are now with God.

In a field opposite the War Memorial, there is a low but sturdy stone cross which probably dates from somewhere between the seventh and twelfth centuries. It looks not unlike one I saw at the monastic site of Cooley in the Inishowen Peninsula in Donegal, and if it belongs to the same period it is more likely to be closer to the earlier rather than the later date suggested above. In mediaeval times other pillar-stones defined the sanctuary or place of refuge for people in trouble with the law.

Now that I had reached the focal point of my pilgrimage, anything else could be considered a bonus. The bonuses were not at all insignificant and the final one was a truly great privilege.

As the evening was pleasant and sunny, I decided to walk to the Tirefour broch which stood out on a ridge by the east coast of the Island. The map indicated that it was a considerable distance by road, but geographically it was fairly close. I opted for the direct approach and, having negotiated some rough terrain and a deep valley, as well as barely escaping the unwelcome attentions of a savage dog, I arrived at this ancient stone fort which overlooks St Moluag's Bay, the very place where, according to tradition, the saint had landed in AD 562.

The next thing to exercise my mind was how to get back home without further risk of encountering the dog. I could see him in the distance patrolling the very territory I had hoped to traverse. Tired though I was, I decided to take a long roundabout way towards the north end of the island which ultimately led on to the main road. Having crossed some fields and fences – the law is liberal on trespass in Scotland – I got on to a by-road and crunched along in my strong shoes. I kept to the grass margin when passing dwelling houses in the hope that sleeping dogs would lie, and in fact I saw one do just that.

The longer route had one possible advantage. It was in the direction of St Moluag's Chair. I dreamt but dared not hope. Finally, when I got on to the main road, I hailed a passing land-rover and asked the driver if St Moluag's Chair was to the left or to the right. He assured me that it was just down the road to the left and offered me a seat as he was passing that way. Gratefully I accepted. In the twinkling of an eye we were there. The driver now offered to wait while I looked at this treasured rock-seat of the island's patron. Having taken a photograph of it, I resumed my seat in the land-rover. As we sped along in the direction of Fiona's home, the driver – an Englishman who had fallen in love with the area – indicated a house on the right where the keeper of St Moluag's Staff lived. I couldn't believe my luck. I was only hours on Lismore and I had already seen the monastic site of Moluag as well as Moluag's Bay, Moluag's Seat, and now there was the possibility of seeing Moluag's Staff.

My driver left me outside Fiona's house. There on the roadside was Colin Rowan and young Christopher with shinty sticks in their hands, on their way to have a game. Colin told me to go inside and have some dinner which they had kept for me. He was friendly and talkative. This was not the kind of man I had first met. Later in the evening as we relaxed by the fire I learned that the initial tension at my arrival was due to the fact that Fiona's husband was fed up of his kind-hearted and lovely wife bringing home strays and wanderers and lost souls, and I was the last straw!

After the meal I sat down and rested after the vigorous and exhilarating evening walking the island. Eventually, of course, the question arose as to who I was and what I was doing in the place. Aware that there are no Catholics living in Lismore I said, 'Don't jump out the window when I tell you.' Fiona assured me that she wouldn't. 'I'm a Catholic priest and monk,' said I. This statement was received calmly and, inevitably, led my hosts to pursue a conversation on the nature and role of religion and the meaning of human existence. Soon we were joined by Mark Willis, the son of the retired teacher who had befriended me on the ferry. Mark was in his kilt on his way to the *céilídh*. We contrasted in height. This caused some inoffensive merriment at our expense. Most people fall short of my six foot seven inches!

Mark had a bottle of whiskey so as not to arrive at the celebration empty-handed. There is no pub in the island but neither is there a shortage of liquor. An attempt had been made to get a pub licence but it was turned down by the community council on the grounds that it would surely change the culture and character of Lismore. It was felt that, with a pub, everything would gradually focus on it. Without a pub people have to be more creative and inventive in their community life. And so indeed they seem to be, for Lismore has its music and dancing, its Gaelic songs and ballads, keep fit classes, bowls and other communal activities and recreations.

The *céilídh* was well under way when we got there. The island hall was bedecked with balloons and multi-coloured streamers. Most of the menfolk were in their kilts and the ladies in graceful tartan dress. There was food and drink for everybody. The dancing was joyous, the music entrancing. The Isle of Skye is famous for good piping, and the Skye piper who entertained us in Lismore was a credit to his island tradition, as were the rest of the Skye musicians. The crowd rose to the music: young and old stepped it out on the floor at a challenging pace as they blithely and lightly interpreted the steps and figures of the Canadian Barn Dance, The Dashing White Sergeant, Strip the Willow, and the rest of Scotland's marvellous dancing repertoire. In the midst of it all there came an announcement: 'A small lady's watch has been handed in.' Amid much hilarity, a formidable and amply endowed woman stepped forward to claim it. The speaker hurriedly rephrased his statement but it was too late. His correct English was drowned in laughter.

Fiona introduced me to several people and, after that, I was on my own to enjoy the evening. It was good to have the opportunity of a chat with people of Lismore and neighbouring Appin and elsewhere. On learning that I was a Catholic priest and monk, several people asked if I had seen 'the college'. This was a reference to the Catholic Seminary for Scotland which was located in Lismore during the years 1803-1829. Another man, conscious of the fact that there are no Catholics on the island, said to me, 'Why did you stay away for so long?' The heat and passion of Reformation days had cooled. People could talk again, could ask questions, could wonder about the vague roots of divisions. Were we not all human, Christian, and Celtic, inheritors of a common language and tradition so much alive in the sounds and movements all around us in the hall that night? I was on an island where the people are proud of my fellow countryman and their revered patron, St Moluag. Why indeed, had I stayed away so long – I, the Catholic Church?

Among the gathering was the keeper of St Moluag's Staff or *Bachuil*. I was assured that he would be happy to let me see this prized relic which has, with the exception of an accidental sojourn at Inverary Castle, been carefully guarded by the Livingstone family of Lismore. At an appropriate moment I was introduced to the keeper of the Staff, the Baron of Bachuil. He graciously invited me to come and see it and we arranged for ten o'clock on the following morning. Would the *céilídh* be over by then? Just about! On inquiring into local custom in this regard I was told that it would go on until three or four o'clock in the morning, but that if the musicians were staying on the island they would repair to a private house where the show would go on. Well, on learning that the musicians were staying on the island, I abandoned the entertainment at 1.00am and retired to bed, feeling more than satisfied with the day that had passed and excited at the prospects of the morrow.

I was the first astir in the morning and quietly slipped out of the house at 8.30 o'clock. It was raining. I had no rain gear and miles to walk. But I did not hesitate. The opportunity to view the Staff of St Moluag would not come again in a hurry and inclement weather was not going to deprive me of it. Boldly I faced into the rain, getting wetter and wetter as I went. Unsure of the exact house, I knocked and waited at more than one door, until finally, as luck would have it, I got a reply from Duncan MacGregor, a farmer, who years earlier had been on his honeymoon in Lismore Mochuda, Co Waterford. He directed me aright so that shortly before ten o'clock, soaked to the skin, I arrived at the home of Alastair Livingstone, Baron of Bachuil.

His wife, who was about to depart on an errand, invited me in and suggested that I remove my sodden anorak. The Baron soon appeared and welcomed me most graciously, inviting me to have tea and giving me one of his own pullovers to wear. He then proceeded to tell me the story of the Pastoral Staff of Saint Moluag.

In the course of history it has been variously referred to as the *Magnum Baculum* (Great Staff), the *Bachuil Mór* (Illustrious Staff), the *Bachuil Búidhe* (Yellow Staff) and, curiously in view of its shape, the *Camán Óir* (Golden Hurling stick/Shinty stick). It is a fine sturdy blackthorn crosier but looks incomplete as if the lower part had been broken off. It now measures 33 inches in length. At one time it was encased in metal, and pockmarking on the stick may indicate that it was studded with jewels. Some fragments of metal still adhere to it.

The Baron told me that the staff is in the family's keeping from time immemorial. The family name had originally been MacDhúnshléibhe (MacLea) but, for some únknown reason, many of the house had changed to Livingstone between 1650 and 1750. A Lion Court judgement in 1950 declared that the custodian of the staff is the co-arb of Saint Moluag and a baron in the Baronage of Argyll and the Isles. Having discoursed on the history of the *Bachuil*, the Baron invited me to come and view it in an adjoining room where it was encased in a wall-shrine behind bullet-proof glass. I contemplated it for a while. Then, placing my hand on the glass, I prayed silently. On observing me do this, Alastair Livingstone, Baron of Bachuil, asked if I would like to touch the staff itself. I assured him that I would love to but that I did not dare ask such a favour. He unlocked the shrine and handed me the *Magnum Baculum*. In a pilgrimage with many high and beautiful moments, this was the ultimate. I felt that St Moluag was taking a very active interest in my outing to Lismore.

The sixth-century crosier was heavy for its size and very solid. I asked my host if I might photograph it. He offered to take a picture of me holding it. We proceeded to the front door where the baron braved the rain and photographed me standing in the doorway holding the ancient relic.

My holding of the *Bachuil* was brief and without risk. But, the Baron told me, a previous keeper in the nineteenth century had loaned it to the Duke of Argyll, who brought it to Inverary Castle. Despite constant representations it was not returned for 124 years! Finally, on 4 January, 1974, Duke Ian Campbell restored it to its rightful keepers in Lismore.

When I took my leave of the Baron, he insisted that I continue to wear the dry pullover and that Fiona would return it to him in due time. I gladly accepted the kind offer and departed. The road was long and it was still raining. But God and St Moluag were on my side. I hadn't gone very far when Archie McCaul pulled up in his car and offered me a lift. Archie is bilingual, so between Gaelic and English and the *céilídh* the night before, we weren't short of conversation. Besides, he told me that he was going to Ireland on holidays the following week and that he hadn't been there since his honeymoon twenty-nine years previously.

On my return to Rowan's house, Fiona was up and about and offered me breakfast. But the ferry was sailing at 11.45am, so breakfast was reduced to a hurried cup of tea and a mouthful of toast. I divested myself of the Baron's pullover, extended a sincere thanks to the members of the household and set my face towards Achnacrois and the Oban ferry. In view of the richness of my experience on the island, it was difficult to credit that I had only set foot on 'Lismore in Alba' less than twenty-four hours previously.

CHAPTER 4

From Cormac the Sailor
to
George Mackay Brown

The Orkney Islands are separated from the north-eastern coast of Scotland by the turbulent Pentland Firth. The archipelago is comprised of some seventy islands, many of which are uninhabited. On my first visit to the islands their beauty and fertility surprised me. Far from the barren mountain and moorland which I had expected, large tracts of grassland met my gaze, with herds of cattle and sheep, and grain and root-crops in abundance. Fish are plentiful in the islands' fresh water lakes – and fishing is free! Partly due to the absence of predatory animals such as foxes and badgers, there is also an abundance of bird-life, among them some rare species. A unique and surprising feature of Orkney bird life is the high level of alcoholism among the seagulls! This, the tour guide informed us on one occasion, is due to their habit of imbibing free drink from a stream which twice-weekly conveys the washings of the Highland Park distillery to the sea.

However, my chief reasons for visiting Orkney were a man long dead, a living poet and a cathedral. The man long dead was Cormac O'Lehane the sailor, an Irish monk of the sixth-century, a native of County Cork who had joined Colmcille (Columba) on Iona. Later he returned to his native land to became abbot of the Columban monastery at Durrow, Co Laois. Having resigned as abbot he took to the seas again, and on one of his many voyages, fetched up in Orkney. St Adamnán, in his *Life of Colmcille*, describes Cormac as 'a truly pious man, who not less than three times went in search of the desert in the ocean, but did not find it'. I spoke to several Orcadians about my fellow Irish monk but failed to find any glimmer of recognition at the mention of his name.

As with Cormac, there is in my own blood something of that spirit of adventure common to most Celts, and it was that that first lead me to Orkney. My pilgrimage began at John o' Groats, that remote spot at the tip of Scotland where an enterprising Dutchman named John de Groot set up a ferry-service to the islands in the late fifteenth century, at a cost of four pence a trip. According to the folk tradition, this four-penny coin subsequently became known as a 'groat.' John is also said to have showed enterprise in the management of family relationships. When his large family quarrelled over precedence, he built an octagonal house with an octagonal dining table so that each member of the querulous household might have a separate entrance and nobody could claim to sit at the head of the table.

The journey from John o' Groats to Orkney takes about forty minutes on the ferry. The Pentland Firth is rarely at rest as it daily channels vast volumes of water from the North Sea into the Atlantic Ocean and back again. Strong winds can further aggravate the firth and add to the perils of seafarers. Naval strategy in World War II caused five of the southern Orkneys to be linked by causeways known as *The Churchill Barriers,* so that having landed at Burwick, one may travel by land through South Ronaldsay, Burray, Glimps Holm, Lambholm, and Hrossey. This latter, 'horse island,' is now generally referred to as the Orkney Mainland.

As one progresses north from island to island it becomes more and more evident that one is leaving Celtic Scotland behind. Place-names are mostly Norse and this is nowhere more evident than in the names of the islands themselves, most of which end in 'say,' 'ey,' 'ay,' or 'a,' which in Old Norse means 'island'. Bird-watchers, too, quickly realise that they are in a Nordic world. Instead of familiar terms such as oyster catcher, shag and fulmar, Orcadians speak of shalder, scarf and mallimack.

Like so many island people, the inhabitants of the Orkneys are of mixed blood. Archaeological remains would seem to indicate a Mediterranean origin for the first settlers. After them came Picts, Celts, Norse, Scots. The Orkneys have hosted vast numbers of army and navy personnel during two world wars. The North Sea oil industry brings many to her shores today, and no doubt Orcadians

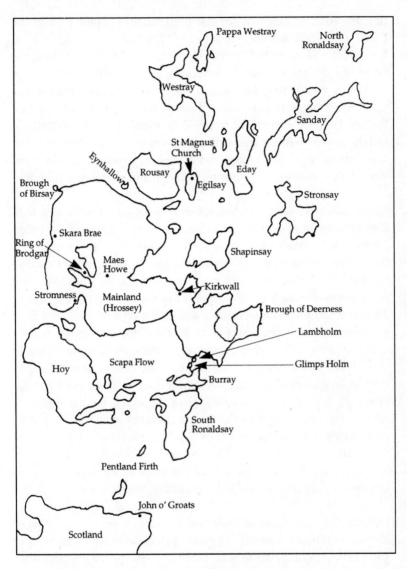

have always attended to victims of the cruel sea, burying the dead and integrating survivors. Of all settlers, the Norse have most indelibly left their stamp on Orkney – a factor which made my Celtic pilgrimage all the more difficult.

Before leaving for the Orkneys, I did some research on the life of Cormac. What I found was meagre enough, but it was sufficient to

fire me with enthusiasm for the pilgrimage. I found that in the
Celtic Christian tradition Cormac O'Lehane is best known as
Cormac the Sailor or St Cormac. He seems to have been born in the
heart of Co Cork around the beginning of the sixth century. From
his youth, we are told, he combined a strong religious sense with a
spirit of daring enterprise and a passion for the sea. It is likely that
he first became a monk at Colmcille's monastery of Durrow, Co
Offaly. It is also likely that Colmcille later appointed him abbot of
that monastery. Surviving references in ancient manuscripts
describe Cormac as an anchorite, a bishop and a monastic founder.

Sixth-century Ireland, to which Cormac belonged, was blessed with
the enthusiasm of a young and vigorous church. Irish monks sailed
north, south, east and west, usually in search of the solitude of a
desert island, but often too in search of the elusive Land of Promise.
Cormac the Sailor seems to have combined both objectives and
made several voyages in the hope of finding 'a desert in the ocean',
as Adamnán puts it, or perhaps stumbling on that land which so
preoccupied his contemporary, St Brendan the Navigator, who is
credited with discovering America. At any rate, Cormac made at
least three unsuccessful attempts to find his heart's desire. St
Adamnán quotes Colmcille, who was gifted with second sight, for
one such failure: 'Cormac going again to search for the desert, is
now embarking from that district which lies beyond the river Moy,
and is called Eirris Domno; nor shall he find this time what he
seeks; and for no other fault than because he has taken into his ship
to accompany him, a monk who is going away, against rule, without the consent of a certain religious abbot, his superior.'

Despite the vagueness of historical references, we can be reason-
ably certain that Colmcille assigned St Cormac to lead a mission to
the Orkneys. Adamnán tells us that on a visit to king Brude Mac-
Maelchon at Inverness, Colmcille had come into contact with the
leader of the Orkney people and obtained a safe-conduct for
Cormac and his fellow monks. That safe-conduct was their salvation, as Adamnán testifies:

> At another time, a soldier of Jesus Christ, named Cormac ...
> made a second attempt to discover a desert in the ocean. He had
> sailed far from the land over the boundless ocean, when St

Columba, who was then staying in Drum Alban, recommended him in the following terms to the chief of the Orkney Islands, in presence of king Brude: 'Some of our brethren have lately set sail to discover a desert in the pathless sea; should they happen after many wanderings to come to the Orkneys, direct this chief, whose hostages are in your hands, to take measures that no evil shall befall them.' The saint recommended this precaution, because he knew that after a few months Cormac would arrive at the Orkneys. And so it came to pass, and to this timely recommendation of our saint, Cormac owed his escape from impending death.

It is possible that it was Cormac who established Christianity among the Orcadians, for there is a tradition that Irish monks, following the rule of Colmcille, worked in the islands in the sixth century. These 'papae' (fathers) were still on the islands when the Norse began their settlements.

Due to lack of archaeological investigation, our knowledge of early Christianity in the Orkneys is scanty, but evidence points to the presence of Celtic hermits and monastic communities there as early as the seventh century at least. On the Orkney Mainland, Corn Holm in Deerness is considered to be a monastic or eremitical settlement of eighth-century date. Further investigation of sites on the islands of Hoy, Sanday, South Ronaldsay, Flotta and many others may yet enhance our understanding of the advance of Christianity on the islands.

The Brough of Deerness, on the eastern side of the Mainland, is a remote promontory difficult of access. There is no certainty as to the identity and date of the settlement there. Iron age fort? Early Christian monastery? Norse settlement, lay or monastic? – all have been suggested. While there is no doubt as to the Norse presence there, it is unclear as to whether a tenth-century chapel predated their arrival; and judging from the eminent suitability of the Brough for prayer and contemplation, it is not difficult to believe that Irish monks were there centuries earlier.

In *An Autobiography*, the poet Edwin Muir, who was born on a farm

in Deerness, credits Cormac the Sailor with the building of the little
stone chapel on the Brough. Then, in a flight of fancy, propelled by
the knowledge that his mother's maiden name was Elizabeth
Cormack, he wonders if the maternal family tree has the saint as its
root. Whatever St Cormac might think of Muir's historical and
genealogical musings, he would surely be touched by George
Mackey Brown's poem *Cormac the Sailor*:

Listen to Cormac the sailor.
He is bent over a harp. He sings.

'When I see the cloud on the hill
I give praise to God.

When I see the sun on the many waters
The round ocean
And the quiet circle of the well
And in the rushing burn
I give praise to God.

I travelled in a ship from Ireland.
I stood in the warehouses
And discussed cargoes and bills-of-lading.
I entered houses
Where there was music, dancing, and verse.
Those things entranced me. Now
The lamp and the jar are lost in light,
I give praise to God.

In middle-Europe I woke from long sleep.
This harp stood at the wall.
Who left it there, an angel?
I give praise to God.

I have known praise and blame.
I have sat at the fire of a good woman
And have eaten her bread.
I have sat, darkling, in a place of bone.
I sailed back over the ocean.
Near a spring of clear water, my childhood,
Continually now *Laus Deo* I sing

When I hear thunder, or raindrops

I give praise to God.
I am an old man now, in a hood.
My fingers are twisted
And I have small taste for wine or fish
But more and more urgently
As days and months and seasons pass
As I see my skull in a stone that shines after rain
O clear and pure as larks in a blue morning
I sing, *Deo gratias.'*

At the further end of the Mainland, on the tidal island known as the Brough of Birsay, there is evidence of a Celtic settlement beneath the Viking-age buildings. Among the archaeological discoveries made here are an early Christian graveyard with a retaining wall, as well as the remains of domestic buildings and, under the later Viking church, some walling which may have been an early Christian chapel. It is too premature to pronounce with certainty on the religious or secular nature of the settlement, but the semi-insular nature of the Brough itself makes it the dream location for Celtic monks looking for 'a desert in the ocean'. Archaeologists are of the opinion that any monks that might have been there left in a hurry, most likely because of Viking marauders. Some three kilometres from the site, an elaborate wooden box containing wood-worker's tools was discovered. This is thought to date from about the year AD 800.

The church of St Magnus on the island of Egilsay is like an enlarged version of 'St Kevin's Kitchen' in Glendalough, Ireland, while the name of the island probably derives from the Irish word *'eaglais'* plus the Norse *'ey'* which, taken together, mean 'Church Island.' The ruins of a church on the island of Eynhallow are traceable to the twelfth century at least, but with a name like Eynhallow (*Eyin-Helga* = Holy Island) this, too, may well be a Celtic monastic or eremitical foundation which the settling Norse came to appreciate as a holy place. Right through the middle ages and up to the eighteenth-century, pilgrims made their way to the chapel of St Triduana, a Celtic nun, on the island of Papa Westray. Down by the shore from St Bonifacekirk on the same island is Munkerhouse, where once stood another Celtic monastery of perhaps sixth-century date. At the kirk

itself were discovered Celtic crosses carved on stone. And the name
of the entire island, Papa Westray, is in itself a likely indication of
the presence of Celtic monks (Papa Westray, 'West Island of the
Priests').

Since most early Christian Celtic sites have virtually nothing visible
remaining, the pilgrim is almost forced into the very atmosphere
which drew the founding monks and hermits to their particular
locations – the silence, the stillness, the sheer loveliness which so
often surrounds these hallowed places. On such sites, even today,
the land, the sea, the beauty, the 'desert in the ocean,' induces a
spirit of contemplation. Almost unintentionally one finds oneself
communing with that God who is so elusive in a high-speed clam-
orous world.

The Orkneys were in Celtic hands for centuries before and after the
arrival of St Cormac. There is a degree of uncertainty as to where he
found 'the place of his resurrection'. Some claim that he was laid to
rest at Kilmacharmaig on Ellanmore Island in Kintyre. There he had
certainly made a foundation; and there stands the remains of an old
church dedicated to his memory. But the weight of opinion is in
favour of Durrow. And did not Colmcille once prophesy that
Cormac would return to that monastery and end his days there? As
with St Moluag of Lismore, a fragment of Cormac's crozier, now
known as the 'Crozier of Durrow,' survived and is preserved in the
National Museum of Ireland in Dublin. This is a relic of particular
interest as it is believed to have originally belonged to St Colmcille
himself, the founder of Durrow, and to have been presented by him
to Cormac.

Celtic pilgrim though I was, my Orkney journeys would have been
far less enriching had I ignored other influences on the islands, particularly those of the Norse. So, having satisfied myself as to the
comings and goings of Cormac the Sailor and his numerous and
nameless companions, I opened my eyes to a wider vision.

A storm in 1850 washed and blew the sand off what must be one of
the world's most interesting archaeological sites, the neolithic village of Skara Brae on the Orkney mainland. Orcadians are quick to

point out that the construction of this village was completed before the pyramid builders set to work in Egypt. Not far distant, between the Lochs of Stenness and Harray, is the spectacular Ring of Brodgar, a massive stone circle 340 feet in diameter. Of the original sixty upright monoliths, thirty-six are still standing. Within sight of this impressive monument are many other outstanding archaeological sites, the most notable of which is the Maes Howe Chambered Tomb.

After more than a thousand years of Celtic occupation, the Orkneys were subjected to yet another strand of colonisation, this time by pagan Vikings from Scandinavia. Around the year AD 800, these began to expand westwards towards the Scottish islands and mainland, towards the Faroes and Iceland, towards the Isle of Man and Ireland. From the frequent sad references in those Irish monastic chronicles that somehow escaped their savage burning and destruction, one can glimpse the horror, the slaughter, the mayhem that accompanied the Viking raids and conquests.

The settlement of the Vikings in Orkney, and their subsequent adoption of Christianity, was probably no exception to the general pattern. Earl Sigurd of Orkney fought on the side of the Danes at the battle of Clontarf in AD 1014. He was a nominal Christian but as his end drew near he was happier listening to the old pagan Norse sagas, something which traditional Gaelic Catholic Celts might not necessarily see as a renunciation of Christianity. His son, Thorfinn the Mighty, was a Christian and on good terms with king Macbeth of Scotland. In fact it is probable that they made a pilgrimage to Rome together.

The Earldom of Orkney evolved in the process of time. It included the Shetlands and extended beyond the Islands to Caithness on the Scottish mainland. With the fortunes of war it expanded and contracted in the usual way and at one time included the Isle of Man. In the early twelfth-century it passed into the joint rule of two cousins, Magnus and Haakon, both grandsons of Thorfinn. The cousins quarrelled. An attempt was made at reconciliation. Both men met on the island of Egilsay on Easter Monday, April 16, probably in the year AD 1117. Haakon did not come in good faith and, though he would have been satisfied with stripping his co-earl of power and title as well as maiming him for life, he seems to have yielded to pressure from his more powerful supporters to have his cousin murdered. Magnus died from a single axe-blow which split his scull. The body was taken to the mainland and laid to rest in the church which his grandfather, Thorfinn, had built at Birsay. People came on pilgrimage to the tomb of the fallen earl. Miracles followed. Magnus was acclaimed a saint and martyr.

A roofless twelfth-century church, with its Irish-style round tower at the west end, still stands on Egilsay. It is Orkney's most conspicuous landmark for seafarers, but whether it is the church in which Magnus prayed before his violent death, or a church built on the site of his slaying, or neither, is not known. (A cenotaph was erected some distance away in 1937 to commemorate the 800th anniversary of the founding of St Magnus Cathedral, Kirkwall, and to mark a spot on the island of Egilsay where, a tradition maintains, the martyrdom took place.) Despite the events in Egilsay on that fateful day in April, Earl Haakon lived on to recover the esteem of his people. His initial insecurity showed itself in vindictiveness towards the followers of Magnus, but in time he repented, made a pilgrimage to Rome and the Holy Land, and in his latter years earned the reputation of being a good ruler. Haakon's son, Paul, succeeded to the Earldom.

Meanwhile, over in Norway, a charming nephew of St Magnus, a son of his sister, was showing great promise as an athlete, poet, scholar, musician, wit, and chess-player. The king of Norway granted him his murdered uncle's inheritance in Orkney. Urged on by his father, and adopting the name Rognvald (Ronald), he made a bid to take possession. The first attempt failed. On the advice of his father, Kol, the young man prayed to St Magnus for help. He also made a vow that if he were successful he would build a magnificent stone church in Kirkwall and dedicate it to the memory of Earl Magnus. Success crowned his second attempt.

True to his vow, two decades after the murderous events on Egilsay, Earl Rognvald laid the foundations of a church in Kirkwall which would perpetuate the sacred memory of his uncle. The martyr's relics were translated from Birsay to Kirkwall. The bishop of Orkney consented to abandon his cathedral in Birsay in favour of making the new church his seat or *cathedra*. Thus Kirkwall cathedral, which enshrined the relics of St Magnus, became a focus of pilgrimage from far and near.

Rognvald was a pious man – at least to the extent that one can juxtapose *'pious'* and *'Viking.'* He himself combined both terms by going on a crusading pilgrimage to the Holy Land which lasted from AD 1151-54 and during which he visited Jerusalem, Constantinople and Rome. He set out with fifteen ships, one of which was commanded by William, bishop of Orkney, known in tradition as *William the Old* since he reigned as bishop for sixty-six years. On the route the old Viking temptations proved too much for the pilgrims. They plundered in Spain, collected booty, took captives, sold slaves, had the occasional orgy, got to Jerusalem, and finally returned home bearing their palm branches like any good Holy Land pilgrims of the day. In 1158, while in Caithness, Rognvald was brutally done to death by some of his own relatives. He was buried in the cathedral he had founded and, like his uncle before him, he, too, was declared a saint of God. He may not have been perfect but the Orkneyinga Saga says of him that he was 'a friend in need to many a man, liberal in money matters, equable of temper, steadfast in friendship, skilful in all feats of strength and a good skald' (i.e. poet).

Beyond the shadow of a doubt his outstanding legacy is St Magnus Cathedral, Kirkwall. It is surely the jewel of the Orkneys. As with the other wonderful mediaeval cathedrals across the Continent of Europe, that of St Magnus took decades to build and has undergone extension and alteration from time to time in the centuries following. In the building of those monuments to faith, journeymen masons and craftsmen as well as local labour were employed. Rognvald, it would seem, drew especially on the expertise of the Durham school of masons. The red sandstone ashlar blocks are native to the area and appropriately coloured for a martyr's memorial. The use of a certain amount of yellow sandstone relieves the eye and enhances the overall appearance of the building. The twelfth-century being a time of architectural development, Kirkwall cathedral reflects both the older heavy Romanesque arches and the lighter soaring Gothic. For the most part, the cathedral escaped the iconoclasm of the sixteenth-century Reformation in Scotland.

In 1848 the remains of William the Old were discovered in the cathedral. This was truly fortunate as William occupied the See of Orkney during many of the most significant events in the twelfth century. Not only had he moved his *cathedra* to Kirkwall, but he is also thought to have been the builder of the bishop's palace there.

During a major renovation of the cathedral in the year 1919, the relics of St Magnus were accidentally discovered lodged in one of the large rectangular piers of the south arcade of the choir. The box which contained the bones is now in Tankerness House Museum just across the street from the cathedral, but the bones themselves, including the scull cleft by the death-wound, were restored to their resting place. The spot is marked by a plaque.

A similar find of human bones was made in another pillar in the early nineteenth century but it was not until 1925 that they were finally recognised as the relics of St Rognvald. These too are marked by a plaque, the inscription on which reads: 'St Rognvald+ Within this pillar lie the remains of Rognvald, Kol's son, Earl of Orkney, who founded this cathedral in 1137. Warrior, Navigator, Skald+. He was assassinated at Calder, Caithness on August 20, 1158. Canonised 1192.' Thus the relics of both the founder and the patron of St Magnus Cathedral, together with the mortal remains of its first bishop are still within its walls – a rare and wonderful reality in view of Scotland's troubled religious and political history.

Moving from the high middle ages to the twentieth-century, Orkney has another treasure for the pilgrim: *The Italian Chapel*. It was built during World War II by the hundreds of Italian prisoners-of-war who were captured during the North African campaign and assigned to the Orkneys to work on the construction of the Churchill Barriers. The Barriers were designed to increase protection by totally blocking the four eastern exits from Scapa Flow. The flow itself is a natural harbour capable of providing anchorage for more ships than any nation or combination of nations is liable to muster at any one time. During the first world war it was headquarters for the British Grand Fleet. It was from there that Lord Kitchener – who had lured so many young men to their death through the famous poster – sailed out to his own death when *HMS Hampshire* struck a mine on 5 June, 1916. It was into Scapa Flow that the defeated German High Seas Fleet, the *Hochseeflotte*, sailed in late November 1918. It was there at noon on the 20th of that same month that its commander, Rear Admiral von Reuter, secretly gave orders for the simultaneous scuttling of every ship in the entire fleet lest they ever be used against Germany at a later date.

During the second world war, a series of ships – discarded merchant vessels for the most part – were sunk across the four eastern exits of Scapa Flow to prevent any enemy ingress. However, a daring and enterprising German named Gunther Prien, having carefully assessed the situation, judged that he could navigate his U-boat through the block-ships at an exceptionally high tide and in otherwise favourable conditions. He hadn't long to wait. On 14 October, 1939, he made his death-dealing voyage into Scapa Flow. *HMS Royal Oak* lay at anchor with fourteen hundred men aboard. He sank it, with the loss of 833 lives, and made a quick escape through the same route by which he had entered. On foot of this embarrassing incident, the British prime minister ordered the complete sealing off of the four eastern entrances to the Flow; hence the Churchill Barriers.

The Italians who were assigned to the task of building the barriers were a dedicated, creative and talented bunch who, though prisoners in the body, were free in spirit. The bleak compound where they lived in thirteen huts was officially known as Camp 60. In this muddy and miserable place, there gradually appeared concrete pathways, grass, flowers. The prisoners established a little recreation room with a concrete billiard table and even set up a theatre, complete with sets. One of the prisoners, Domenico Chiocchetti, a high quality artist, made a statue of St George out of concrete and wire. One thing they still sorely missed: a chapel.

A fortunate combination of events and personnel led to the acquisition of two Nissen huts in the latter part of 1943, and, propelled principally by the genius of Chiocchetti, a chapel began to take shape. The raw materials were raw in every sense of the word. The outcome is a monument to human genius. It also stands as an impressive alternative to consumerism. In an age when the resources of the earth are being so mindlessly exploited, it is salutary to sit in the Italian Chapel and contemplate how much can be done with so little. The builders had two galvanised huts, a certain amounts of concrete, and an unpromising collection of scrap material – mainly bits of barbed wire and discarded tin cans from the kitchen. They also pooled their tiny personal allowances to buy paint, curtains and other church appurtenances. With these very limited resources, the artists got to work and frescoes appeared in all their loveliness – the cherubim and the seraphim, the Madonna and child, St Francis of Assisi and St Catherine of Sienna. This chapel was becoming a home from home and a focal point for the faith and yearnings of the exiled Catholics. The thorn-crowned head of Christ was represented, in concrete and wire, over the entrance door. From the same material was made an altar, an altar-rail and a holy water stoup. To separate the sanctuary from the nave, an ornate rood-screen was conceived and executed by a skilled iron-monger named Palumbo. For his work of art he used pieces of scrap and the tin cans discarded each day by the kitchen staff.

At the same time, the back-breaking work of making and laying down the quarter of a million tons of stone and rock for the Churchill Barriers continued. In places the sea-bed was at a depth of fifty-nine feet. This had to be filled in with stone. The barrier was then topped off with a further 66,000 concrete blocks, each of which weighed either five or ten tonnes. As things turned out, both the Barriers and chapel were not long completed when the war came to an end. The prisoners returned to Italy but their handiwork remained.

By the late 1950s, the Italian Chapel was still a cause for wonder. It was also showing signs of wear. At this point Signor Chiocchetti returned from Italy and spent some weeks restoring the little mas-terpiece. On 10 April, 1960, a rededication ceremony was held. Fr Whitaker, SJ, the then parish priest of the Orkneys, celebrated the Eucharist and concluded his sermon thus:

Of the buildings clustering on Lambholm in wartime only two

remain: this chapel and the statue of St George. All the things which catered for material needs have disappeared, but the two things which catered for spiritual needs still stand. In the heart of human beings the truest and most lasting hunger is for God.

Despite my great interest in Celtic Pilgrimage and the pursuit of Cormac the Sailor; despite my determination to get to Kirkwall Cathedral at some time in my life, what really drove me to the Orkneys for the first time was a dream and a hope: I had a secret ambition to meet the Orcadian writer George Mackay Brown. It was at our monastery in Athenry in the west of Ireland that my con-frère, Fr Dick Tobin, had first introduced me to *An Orkney Tapestry*. I liked it and followed through with *Greenvoe* and others. Here was a writer to whom I could relate, by whom I could be nourished and enriched, a man of spiritual depth and sensitivity, with the breadth of vision and appreciation of life that can only be contained in a humble heart. Oftentimes when reading his books I mused to myself that it would be lovely to meet him face to face and thank him for the joy he had brought me.

It happened that in 1987 a small party of us were travelling by car in Scotland. Officially we had no definite plans as to where we would go, but I had a secret hope that we might get to the Orkneys, and who knows but...! We left Dunfermline one morning and travelled by way of Dunkeld, Dalwhinny and Newtonmore at a leisurely pace, until we eventually arrived at Inverness in the afternoon. After a rest and some sight-seeing, the evening being still young and fine, I suggested that we motor on and stop when we felt the time appropriate. So we did just that, heading north over the Beauly Firth into the Black Isle, on by Dornoch, Brora, Helmsdale. Would we go further? The sun glistened on the placid surface of the North Sea where oil rigs were sucking up the *black gold* from the depths. Yes, we would go further. And we did, through Dunbeath, Lybster, and Wick till we came to John o' Groats, which for us was lands-end.

Early next morning, after some hesitation due to uncertain weather conditions, we embarked on a 'Maxi Day Tour' to the Orkney Islands. My heart beat faster as I saw the realisation of my secret

hope draw closer. By the time we reached Kirkwall, I had made sufficiently bold on the genial coach driver to inquire if he knew where
George Mackay Brown lived. He told me that he lived in Stromness.
My heart sank. We disembarked and visited St Magnus Cathedral.
Now that was a truly good experience, even if I never met Mr
Brown. On board again, the coach operator announced that our
next stop would be Stromness. Not only that but it would be a
major stop. On arrival, I dashed for the tourist office and asked the
lady inside the counter of she knew where George lived. She did.
She even drew a map of how to get there. I hurried my step in the
direction of the house, apprehensive as to whether my secret hope
was to be realised – would he be at home? down by the shore? talking with old sailors at the pier? away 'just for that day only.' I
knocked at the door. No reply. But being a missioner I was used to
knocking on doors, visiting houses and meeting people. I tried the
next door. No reply. And the next. Nothing. I saw a woman across
the court and called out: 'Where could I find George Mackay
Brown?' She was soft-spoken and helpful, 'Open the door and call
him. If he is inside he will answer.' So I did just that and my heart
rejoiced to hear 'Yes?' from an inner room.

I still treasure the ensuing conversation with that gentle, gifted,
saintly man. For years afterwards I planned on a extended stay on
the islands with a view to having more time with him. But when the
opportunity eventually presented itself in June of 1996, George's
own earthly pilgrimage had come to an end. May he rest in peace.

CHAPTER 5

The Faroe Islands
Where the blackbird sings at midnight

Ever since reading Tim Severin's book *The Brendan Voyage*, my heart was set on reaching the Faroes. I wanted to make a pilgrimage to those unmarked islands north of Britain of which the Irish monk Dicuil wrote in AD 825; but unlike Tim Severin I had no wish to travel in the same kind of craft as those early Celtic voyagers did. In the event, however, my determination to go by sea rather than by air was uncomfortably close to the experience of Brendan and his fellow Celtic monks. In fact, I'm convinced that they had a more pleasant outing than my twenty-three hours of sea-sickness on board the *Smyril Line* between Aberdeen in Scotland and Tórshavn in the Faroes.

As fortune would have it, I had acted as chaplain to a 'charismatic weekend' a day or two prior to departure. While I was praying in the chapel, three charismatics descended upon me and asked if I wished to have them pray over me. As I accept prayers from all sources, I gave the go ahead. No sooner had they started than one of them, a Glaswegian, said to me, 'Do you own a boat?' 'No,' I replied. 'Do you have access to a boat?' she persisted. 'No such luck!' said I. Her next utterance came in the form of a statement: 'I can see a boat in stormy seas. It is tossing and rolling and turning upside down. And now I see the waters becoming more calm again and everything is all right.' I was decidedly uncomfortable at this stage and timidly mentioned that I was intent on boarding the *Smyril Line* at Aberdeen and heading for the Faroe Islands on Tuesday morning. This bit of bleating on my part must have come close enough to insulting her as she swiftly and confidently assured me that this vision of hers had nothing to do with such mundane matters as a Scandinavian ferry. This, she insisted, was a manifestation of the power of the Holy Spirit working in me, a revelation of

the wonderful things the Spirit would do in and through me. The
language sounded all too familiar in the context of a charismatic
weekend, and I wasn't convinced. Time would tell. And it did.

The Glaswegian visionary was in reality enjoying what in Gaelic
Scotland is known as 'the second sight'. She was giving me a pre-
view of the journey ahead. The only bit that was wrong – thank God
– was that the ship didn't turn upside down! Aside from that it was
accuracy all the way. My friends, Jamus and Helen Smith, who took
me to the pier in Aberdeen, told me later that they waited until the
ship moved out into the open waters and watched it pitching and
rolling until it went out of sight. The bad weather conditions lasted
for about ten to twelve hours until we were past the Shetlands.
Thereafter the force-nine winds dropped and the seas grew calm
for the remainder of the journey. By the time we reached Tórshavn,
the Faroese capital, all was tranquillity and peace – all except my
poor stomach! At that point, I offered a prayer to the effect that the
good Lord would lead all charismatics to distinguish clearly
between the gift of 'second sight' and the gifts of the Holy Spirit.
Had that distinction been made earlier, I might have taken some
medical precautions with a view to a happier sailing.

At Tórshavn two Franciscan nuns, Sr Cecilia O'Hagan from Newry
and Sr Julian from Belgium, interrupted their work-schedule to
welcome me and show me to my apartment under the new Church
of Our Lady. That church is the only Catholic one in the North
Atlantic and is within the jurisdiction of the bishop of Denmark.
The shortage of priests in his diocese precludes the bishop from
appointing a full-time pastor for the small number of Catholics in
the Faroes. Clergy are flown in from Copenhagen on the basis of a
monthly rota. The opening line of Father O'Flynn, 'Of priests we can
offer a charming variety,' came to mind as Sr Cecilia regaled me
with stories of priests who had served the parish during the first
half of 1995: a pyromaniac, an atheist, a married man, the bishop
himself and, with my arrival, a Celtic monk. I need hardly add that
the pyromaniac has long since abandoned his fiery pursuits and the
atheist his bleak vision but the married man has not abandoned his
wife. By special permission, he is allowed follow the dual vocations
of marriage and priesthood.

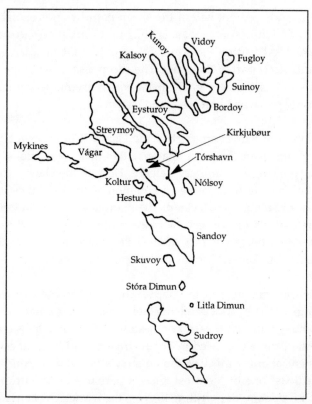

The Faroese archipelago contains 1400 square kilometres of land spread over eighteen mountainous volcanic islands, of which seventeen are inhabited. The islands are separated by deep fjord-like channels and surrounded by the wild Atlantic wave. They lie about half way between Scotland and Iceland, and, thanks to the Gulf Stream, enjoy a relatively mild climate. One is not in 'the land of the midnight sun' but there is no real darkness for a couple of months in summer. The ninth-century Irish scholar, Dicuil, maintained that it was bright enough at this latitude to pick lice off one's companion at midnight! Being as I was without a companion or the need for the above mentioned service, I celebrated the midnight hour by reading my New Testament in the open air.

The Faroe Islands have a population of under 44,000 people and almost twice that number of sheep. It is likely that the islands derive their name from the latter, the Norse *Faereyjar*, meaning

'Sheep Islands.' About half of the sheep population is slaughtered annually and much of the meat is hung up in airy places to dry out. This raw dried mutton – skerpikjoát – provides the people with the most nutritious part of their diet. The sheep also provide the wool, long known as 'Faroese gold,' from which are made the islands' beautifully patterned knit-wear and tartan.

Politically, the Faroes are part of the Danish Commonwealth but enjoy Home Rule in most matters, the main exceptions being finance, policing and military defence. Despite the Danish connection, the Faroese have more in common with their ancestors in Norway and relatives in Iceland. Their language is akin to Icelandic and the dialects of Western Norway, more specifically those districts south of Bergen. In fact, modern Faroese is close to the kind of Norwegian spoken in Norway in the fifteenth century.

Despite the smallness of the population, the Faroese have all the trappings of a fully independent state – their own parliament, cultural centre, national theatre, orchestra, radio and television stations. All of these are based in Tórshavn, the world's smallest capital, where about a third of the country's population reside. The islands boast one of the most ancient parliaments in Europe and one of the most modern fishing fleets in the world. They have opted to stay out of the European Union largely to protect their fishing grounds, because, like their Viking ancestors, the Faroese are a people of the sea; and of all the villages scattered throughout the islands only one is inland.

Fishing is the primary source of employment and income. Their whaling policies and practices bring the islanders into conflict with conservationists, but the Faroese are quick to point out that the pilot whale, which they hunt for food, is not an endangered species. They also maintain that their harvesting of the sea is as normal and humane as farming life in other lands. Whale meat makes up about 10% to 15% of Faroese diet at present. Because of the pollution of the oceans by industrial nations, there are now high levels of toxic chemicals such as DDT and cancer-causing PCBs in the meat, with the result that the Faroese are being advised to reduce their intake of both whale-meat and blubber. It is a hard decision for more rea-

sons than one. The whale has ever been part of their diet and culture. It was often the only meat they had and its very existence is
symbolic of community bonds since the whale hunt, the *grindadráp*,
is a skilled community exercise and the takings are divided not only
among the boat crews but also with every family in the community.

Tórshavn is picturesque. The housing starts right at the harbour
and climbs ever higher into the hillside. The houses are built of
wood, stone, corrugated iron, concrete cladding or combinations of
all four. To colours and colour schemes there is no limit – blue,
white, maroon, black, grey, green, yellow. Most houses are two-
tone but often a third colour or a fourth appears on windows or
roof. The latter is mostly of conventional modern building material,
but the traditional Faroese roof is the green sod and it is retained to
some degree because it is good and reliable. It looks well, too. How
to keep it trimmed during the grass-growing season is a matter of
personal choice. At Patursson's in Kirkjubøur I noted three lambs
happily grazing on the roof of the oldest family residence in Europe.

Added to all this, the Faroese have a national bird – the Oyster
Catcher (*Tjaldur*). Since the bird is a protected species, I thought it
downright bad form for one of them to attack me with all the
viciousness and determination of the Vikings driving off my Celtic
monastic predecessors. After all, I was only a visitor and had no
designs on dethroning him from his privileged status, rare bird
though I might be. What annoyed me most of all was the fact that he
probably winters in Ireland where he is treated with the utmost
respect and appears on ornithological programmes on Irish television. What ingratitude, then, to return in mid-March to his Nordic
habitat, only to behave like any city mugger attacking visitors. By
contrast, the humble blackbird – a direct descendant, surely, of
those same blackbirds that inspired heavenward thoughts in my
sixth-century monastic counterparts – perched himself outside my
basement window at Mariukirkja and sang me to sleep in the twilight hours of midnight and beyond. *Vive le Merle!*

It was the hope of tracing some of the footsteps of those monastic
predecessors of mine that had me on the islands in the first place.
There is no document specifically stating that Celtic monks from

Ireland ever inhabited the Faroes. There is, however, circumstantial evidence pointing to the presence of Irish monastic and anchoretical settlements in the islands for a considerable time prior to the arrival of the Vikings. There are, for example, the descriptions found in the epic voyage associated with St Brendan the Navigator set in the latter half of the sixth century. There is also the evidence of oats being grown in the islands of Mykines, Eysturoy and Suduroy as early as AD 600 – long before Viking times. Furthermore, the cultivated areas were often almost inaccessible slopes facing south and west, the typical locations sought out by Irish hermits. The field-patterns also conform to the early mediaeval in-field type well known in Ireland. Then there is the ancient graveyard in the island of Skuvoy where cross-inscribed stones point to Celtic influence or even Celtic origin.

Several place-names point in the same direction. The topography of the Island of Dímun would suggest that it derives its name from the Irish words *dá*, two, and *muin*, a ridge. Korkadalur in Mykines would seem to derive from the Irish word for oats, *coirce*, and to mean oat-valley. In the old days, the inhabitants of Foula in Shetland referred to oat bread as *korkakost*, from the Irish, *coirce*, meaning 'oats,' and *císte* meaning 'a cake'. The village of Vestmannahovn (now Vestmanna in Streymoy) means 'the harbour of the westmen', indicating arrivals from Ireland or parts of the islands of Britain. Baglahólmur in Suduroy derives from the Irish *bachall*, meaning a walking stick or staff, with particular reference to the crozier of a bishop or abbot. Faroese words incorporating *argi*, *ergi, aergi, airge*, all derive from the same Irish root, *aire*, meaning to care or tend. In the Faroese context, this referred especially to caring for or tending cattle; as for example, in Argir in Tórshavn and Ergidalur in Suduroy. Also associated with cattle are the Irish loan words, 'tarvur' from *tarbh* meaning a bull, and 'blak' from *bláthach*, which in Irish means 'buttermilk' but in Faroese has the more generic meaning of 'sour milk'.

In the Faroes, as in Shetland, Orkney and elsewhere, the word *paper* – meaning priests – often occurs in place-names. Paparokur and Papurshálsur in Streymoy would seem to refer to Irish priests or priest-hermits. But one cannot be quite sure of this because of a play on the words *papar* for priests and *papi* for puffins. Since both priest and puffin tended to occupy the same kind of remote and inaccessible habitats, the Vikings often referred to *papars* as *papi* and *papi* as *papars!* Be that as it may, in Suduroy there is a tradition of holy men (*papar*) living on the island before the Norse. These men were said to possess the power of healing, they had respect for God's creatures great and small, and they confined their food intake to milk, eggs and seaweed – carrigeen moss, dulse and perhaps other edible weed. Their knowledge of the weather and fishing grounds were also matters for wonder. But if these holy men came from Ireland, their knowledge of the weather and the seas were no wonder at all as such knowledge would have been essential to anybody sailing into the uncharted Nordic regions.

Furthermore, Dicuil, the scholarly Irish monk at the imperial court of the Franks in the early ninth century, comments in his *Liber de mensura orbis terrae*, (The Book Concerning the Measure of the World):

> There are many other islands in the ocean to the north of Britain which can be reached from the northern islands of Britain in a direct voyage of two days and nights with sails filled with a continuously favourable wind. A devout priest told me that in two summer days and the intervening night he sailed in a two-benched boat and entered one of them. There is another set of small islands, nearly all separated by narrow stretches of water; in these for nearly a hundred years hermits sailing from our country, Ireland, have lived. But just as they were always deserted from the beginning of the world, so now because of the Northman pirates they are emptied of anchorites, and filled with countless sheep and very many diverse kinds of sea-birds. I have never found these islands mentioned in the authorities.

In my innermost heart, I had set the goal of my Faroese pilgrimage as St Brendan's Bay at Kirkjubøur in the island of Streymoy, right in the middle of the archipelago. Brendan's birth-place and mine are less than thirty miles apart. When I was growing up, his name was a household word because he is both the apostle and patron of our diocese of Kerry, which includes my native Kiskeam in Co Cork. The *Navigatio* or 'Voyage of St Brendan' was an integral part of the culture of the area. Whether the man himself made the journey to America *via* the North Atlantic islands, or whether the *Navigatio* is a literary or liturgical work integrating authentic stories from Celtic monks who ploughed the seas in search of a 'desert in the ocean,' as Adamnán puts it, is not all that important. What is quite evident from reading the *Navigatio,* and from Tim Severin's epic voyage in the mid 1970s, based on the *Navigatio,* is the fact that from a sea-man's point of view there is no contradiction between the text describing the voyage of St Brendan and the capability of a sixth-century type craft to undertake it.

Sister Maria Forrestal from Co Wexford, a member of the Tórshavn Community of the Franciscan Missionaries of Mary, accompanied me on the last stage of my pilgrimage to St Brendan's Bay. A resident of the islands for some years, and an energetic, knowledgeable lady, Sister Maria was a good guide over the mountain pass that leads from Tórshavn to Kirkjubøur and Brandarsvík. Until relatively recently, the only access to Kirkjubøur was either over this mountain pass or by sea.

It was early on a Sunday afternoon, the feast of *Corpus Christi,* when we packed a sandwich or two and set off on foot over the mountain. With us was the resident deacon from the parish. The entrancing beauty of mountain, sky and sea distracted us from aching muscles and tired feet. The well-worn path is punctuated by a series of ancient but well-maintained cairns, so that the pilgrim always has sight of one – a very practical arrangement, especially in a climate where mists, dense fogs and clouds can sweep in from the sea without a moment's notice. We were fortunate, however, in the fact that our journey was made in brilliant sunshine. Rising higher and higher we saw more and more. Into view came several of the islands – Nólsoy, Hester, Koltur, Sandoy and Vágar. Without noticing the two-hour journey, we found ourselves at the *mons gaudi* – the joyful peak from which one sees the pilgrim destination – and looked down with true joy at Kirkjubøur and the little bay named after Brendan. So this green sward between mountain and sea was the centre of church life in the Faroes throughout the Middle Ages! The roofless mediaeval cathedral of St Magnus is there to prove it; so too is the church of St Olaf, now the Lutheran parish church. And there is the bishop's house, presently and for eighteen generations owned by the Patursson family, one of whom – Tróndur – played such a vital role in the success of Tim Severin's voyage. Lapping the shore are the waters of Brandarsvík, those same waters which have washed away all but the last vestiges of a church bearing the name of the saintly Navigator.

In a letter dated May, 1420, the resident bishop, John the German, refers to the fact that this little church of St Brendan was in the process of being built. The fact that it is the smallest and the latest of the churches at Kirkjubøur raises the question of why the bay should be named after it rather than after the much finer and more ancient churches of Magnus or Olaf? Indeed why should it not be called simply Kirkjubøur Bay? As there are no written sources to confirm or deny a relationship to a Celtic settlement, an archaeological dig may throw some light on the situation. Yet even that would be hampered by the fact that the sea has already swallowed up a lot of the evidence, since most of the little church and surrounding graveyard have disappeared beneath the waves. So the question remains as to why Kirkjubøur played such an important role in Faroese life throughout the Middle Ages. Why indeed, if not because of Brendan's visit and monastic settlement?

The Cathedral of St Magnus, begun about AD 1300, was never quite finished, because, it is believed, the people revolted against Bishop Erlendur's fund-raising policies for the project. Known simply as 'The Wall', it has stood roofless for centuries. Among the more notable remaining fragments of the cathedral's furnishings, which still survive in a museum in Copenhagen, are some elaborately carved pine bench ends depicting, among other things, the Virgin and Child, The Visitation, the Twelve Apostles, and the coat of arms of King Erik and Queen Phillipa who ruled Norway in the early fifteenth century. In a surviving lectern panel there is a carving of an abbot, complete with staff, torch and halo – surely Brendan himself?

Partly because of his larger-than-life personality, and partly because of his association with the *Navigatio* epic, the veneration of St Brendan spread not only all over Ireland and Britain but far into the

Continent and the Nordic lands. The *Navigatio* itself was translated into a multitude of European languages and a fragment of it even survives in Old Norse. The saint (c AD 484-577) was born in the vicinity of Tralee, Co Kerry, was fostered according to the Irish custom by the great St Ita of Limerick, and established several monasteries in and out of Ireland. He died at Annaghdown on the shores of Lough Corrib in Co Galway and was buried at Clonfert in the same county. Brendan's grave is still pointed out in front, and a little to the right, of the exquisite Romanesque doorway of Clonfert's mediaeval cathedral.

When the turbulence of the Reformation reached the Faroes, *via* Denmark, in 1538, Kirkjubøur felt the impact most. The seminary was closed, the priests were marginalised, the cult of the saints abandoned. The new Danish Lutheran Liturgy, led by Lutheran ministers, was imposed on the people and the Catholic Church was abolished. Over the years following, the King of Denmark confiscated all the lands that had formerly belonged to the Catholic Church in the Faroes and granted them to his own friends. These favoured occupants became known as *the king's farmers;* and while privately owned lands might be subdivided within families, the king's lands could not. Because of this, the tenants themselves became, in the course of time, a symbol of stability. Marriage alliances between them and the families of Lutheran ministers further consolidated this image. The bulk of people who survived on dwindling properties or without any land at all, tended to become employees and servants of *'the king's farmers'* – much as happened under the landlord system in Ireland, Scotland and elsewhere and at the same time.

Catholicism never regained ground in the Faroes after the Reformation. The country remains predominantly Lutheran. Until the late nineteenth century, the anti-Catholic prejudices and bigotry common to most Nordic and Anglo-Saxon lands in the post-Reformation era were present also in the Faroes. Despite the introduction of religious freedom in 1849, there was only one Catholic resident on the islands at the turn of the century. Now there are about seventy, but these include not only Faroese – who make up about half – but also Polish, Senegalese, Indian, Maltese, Flemish, Irish, English, Danish, Philippino, Indonesian and Croatian. Among other minority religious groups and sects are a strong contingent of Plymouth Brethren, together with Seven Day Adventists, Jehovah's Witnesses, Salvation Army and Bahá'í.

A major step in re-establishing a Catholic presence in the Faroes was taken in 1931. In that year, Cardinal Van Rossum, a Redemptorist like myself, introduced from Belgium into the islands a community of Franciscan Missionaries of Mary. The presence of these Catholic nuns was for long a source of curiosity, as they ran their school and quietly conducted a variety of works of mercy. Now, the Faroese have a better appreciation of them as a community of religious women dedicated to the spirit and values of the gospel of Jesus, and often join them for prayer and reflection. As one Faroese woman put it, 'We know the Bible. We want some Catholic spirituality!'

Ecumenism has its own momentum and requires much patience. God has no clock and his mills grind slowly but surely. While con-celebrating Mass in the beautiful new (1987) Church of Mary in Tórshavn, I listened to the *Corpus Christi* sermon of Bishop Hans Martensen, SJ, and detected a tangible note of hope founded on the belief that with all our mismanagement of human relationships we cannot foul up the ultimate designs of God:

> On this feast of *Corpus Christi* we think of Christ the Risen Lord who is hidden (in the Eucharist), as the One who has overcome death. And we shall adore him and say: 'Truly you are present here, just as truly as you met the disciples after your Resurrection.' And secondly, Christ is here as the One who is the centre of everything – he who gathers all that is scattered: all that is scattered in my own life, in the people I know. Everything is centred and gathered in him. And that which even I forget – sins I have committed, good things I have done – he remembers it all; but he remembers in God. And he gathers together all that is scattered, the living and the dead. Also the fact that we are alive to him who is the first-born of those risen from the dead. And in the end … all mankind, and every man in his death, will see the face of Christ, flow into his heart, and in this way be judged by his mercy. And so in this way we shall celebrate this feast of *Corpus Christi*, and also celebrate it in hope. We are still in this mortal life but he is now in the life of the Resurrection and he says: 'Where I am you also shall be.' Amen.

CHAPTER 6

Islay
and the Kildalton Cross

April 1993 found me working in Kintyre. Fr Joe Naughton, CSSR, and myself had undertaken to conduct the Holy Week ceremonies in the Catholic parish of St Kieran's, Campbeltown, and follow through with a parish mission, i.e. a visitation of all the Catholic homes and a week of church services that gave centrality to preaching. There are less than 450 Catholics in this extensive parish which stretches for thirty or more miles north from the Mull of Kintyre and also includes the large island of Islay. From our Campbeltown base we judged that whatever success we might have on the mainland, a mission in Islay at this time was out of the question because the island is a voyage of some two and a quarter hours from Kennacraig at the top end of the parish. However, we agreed that since it was Eastertime, one of us would pay a short visit to the island and celebrate the Holy Eucharist there. For long I had sought a suitable opportunity of making a pilgrimage to Islay and the Kildalton cross. This was the moment of grace. I knew that my confrère's passion was Manchester United, so there would be no conflict of interest.

Mrs McNeil, who had nursing responsibility for Gigha island, off the coast of Kintyre, was more than generous in providing transport for us during the mission, and she it was who took me to the ferry at Kennacraig where I embarked for Islay. Weather conditions were wintry. The Paps of Jura, at a height of over two and a half thousand feet, were plainly visible among the many peaks and valleys on that rugged island. (By coincidence the Paps of Anann, which dominate the south-western view from my home in Co Cork, are virtually identical in height.) Manannan Mac Lir, the Celtic sea-god, was in no small hurry on that day. The white manes of his horses were all that was visible on the surface of the water as he

drove furiously over the waves. In the prevailing conditions it was easy to see how our Celtic ancestors had personalised the elements and forged a colourful mythology from their surroundings.

A young man named O'Donnell from Dunkineely, Co Donegal, awaited my arrival at Port Ellen. He deposited me in the care of Patricia and Dunstan Gallery at Glenegedale House which was to be my base for the duration of the short visit. The first commitment was to celebrate the Holy Eucharist for the Catholic community. These number about one hundred but the Eucharist is not always uppermost in their minds and we ended up with a dozen or a little less. There is no Catholic church on the island, but thanks to good ecumenical relationships, we celebrated Mass in the little Anglican (Episcopal) Church of St Columba at Bridgend. Despite the numbers, there was music and song to enhance the liturgy of the day; and that day was the Second Sunday of the Easter Season, formerly known as Low Sunday – after the high of Easter itself.

Through both sight-seeing and conversation, Islay was gradually

78 A PILGRIM IN CELTIC SCOTLAND

revealed to me. It is a beautiful island, appropriately styled *Queen of the Hebrides*. It is indeed one of the most beautiful parts of all Scotland and, not surprisingly, hosts some quarter of a million tourists annually. The island has lots of bogs and farmlands as well as lakes, mountains and sea lochs. In winter it is visited by approximately 37,000 geese from Nordic lands. They include two thirds of the world's population of Greenland Barnacle Geese together with Greying and Whitefronts from Greenland and Iceland. These winter visitors are totally oblivious of the controversy surrounding them. Farmers are unhappy with them because they devour such large quantities of grass. (The old Gaelic ratio relating to grazing was eight geese to a cow.) Those who operate the island's seven whiskey distilleries are likewise unhappy because they are not allowed to extend peat cutting where the geese are wont to graze and it is the local peat that gives Islay malts their distinctive flavour. Meanwhile, some naturalists down in London who favoured reintroducing brown bears, wolves and lynx into Britain, suggested that these animals be allowed to roam wild in Islay. The perpetrators of this suggestion must have been blissfully ignorant of the 4,000 people on the island, to say nothing of the 37,000 gaggling geese. The suggestion confirmed my long standing conviction that a combination of goodwill and ignorance is a devastating cocktail.

The coast of Co Antrim is only twelve miles distant from the Mull of Kintyre and the Island of Islay is just about twice that distance from the Irish shore. Little wonder then that from the earliest times there has been a high degree of activity on the seas that divide them. As we saw in an earlier chapter, about the end of the fifth century AD, the sons of Erc – Fergus, Loarn and Angus – left their native Dal Riada in Antrim to carve out a kingdom for themselves on the other side of *Sruth na Maoile*. The result of their efforts was the creation of Scottish Dal Riada, with Fergus established at Dunadd in Knapdale, Loarn at Dunollie in Oban, and Angus in Islay.

Among the early Irish saints associated with Islay are Colmcille, Brendan the Navigator, Maolrubha of Applecross, and one or more of the many St Ronans. I had hardly set foot on the island when I was told of the arrival of St Colmcille on his way to Iona. His initial influence on Islay grew stronger with the passage of time as we

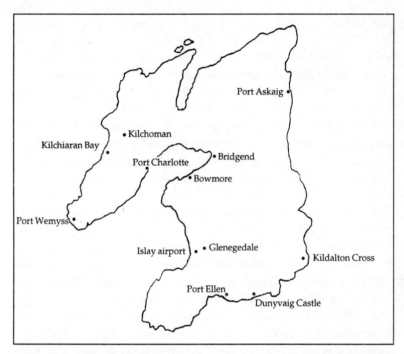

know from the various Columban sites on the island and the fact
that the Iona monks possessed property there throughout the
Middle Ages.

Place-names reveal further saintly influences. Kilchoman was an
early monastic site associated with St Comman, a seventh-century
monk of Iona and brother of the illustrious Abbot St Cuimine,
whose letter to Rome concerning the dating of Easter is of such historical and theological importance. Kilchiaran takes its name from St
Kieran (*alias*, Kenneth, Canice, *Caineach*), a close associate of
Colmcille and his companion on the delicate mission to King Brude
at Inverness. He is patron of Kintyre and has churches dedicated to
him in many parts of mainland Scotland and the islands. His cave-
retreat near Campbeltown is still a place of pilgrimage. Kilarow
keeps the memory of St Maelrubha green in Islay as do several
other dedications throughout the West Highlands. Some disjointed
snippets of history, together with gleanings from the archaeology
and topography of the land, is all that can be retrieved from what
must have been a glorious chapter of Scottish Christianity, so that
one is left to wonder at what was lost.

The Kildalton Cross is generally acknowledged to be the outstanding legacy of the lost centuries. That cross was the goal of my Islay pilgrimage and I was determined to get there if at all possible. The dream might not have been realised were it not for the goodwill of my hosts at Glenegedale House. It was arranged that Dunstan Gallery would drive me. The weather was most inhospitable, being both wild and wet. Dunstan got into his rain-gear while his wife, Patricia, did her best to outfit me in similar attire. During these preparations I noticed what was for me an unusual sight: about one hundred and fifty wild geese grazing in the back garden.

The journey to Kildalton took us first past the airport, then the golf-course, and so to the little village of Port Ellen, built in the early nineteenth century by Walter Frederick Campbell and named after his wife. Walter Frederick was a member of an enlightened and energetic family of Campbell lairds, the progenitor of which was 'Great Daniel' who bought the Island when things were at a very low ebb and, between himself and his successors, turned its fortunes around. It was Daniel who, in 1767, established the first regular boat service to the mainland, and it was Daniel also who built Bowmore village and round church – where there is no corner for the devil to hide! His plan was to establish an urban base for a growing population who found it more and more difficult to make a living off the land. He also built Islay House, and even though it has undergone change and development, the original structure has not been destroyed.

His brother Walter who succeeded him continued the building momentum and added substantial piers at Bowmore and elsewhere. Next came Walter Frederick, and amongst his building projects, aside from Port Ellen, was Port Charlotte, named after his mother, and Port Wemyss, named after his father-in-law. It was the potato famine of 1847 that brought Walter Frederick to grief. Taking no rents from his wretched tenants and continuing to pour money into the provision of their relief, he went bankrupt and the estate changed hands. He lived out his days away from his cherished Islay, and survived on the charity of his friends who had organised a small pension for him. At this point fate took a wonderful turn. Walter Frederick's son John – Iain Óg Ile – having no inheritance awaiting him, embarked on a life-long career of collecting the folk-lore and songs of the Highlands and Islands, and to him Scotland must be forever indebted for the inheritance that he left it.

After Port Ellen, on the road to Kildalton, three of Islay's famous distilleries – Laphroaig, Lagavulin, and Ardbeg – came into view in quick succession. Not being a drinking man myself, I can only take on faith the received tradition among the bacchanalian fraternity that mature single malts from Islay are hard to beat. After all, Islay has been producing whiskey for more than two centuries with a government licence – and for goodness knows how long without it!

Apart from the distilleries, something else in the vicinity caught my eye – Holy Hill Fort (*Dún Náomhaig*). This was no ordinary fort, but Dunyveg Castle. It was from this spot, and the lake-island and castle of Finlaggan, that the Lords of the Isles governed. It all started towards the end of the Viking era when, in 1079, Godfrey – known in Manx tradition as Orry – became King of Man. Secure in his position, Orry spent a lot of his time on Islay and may well have been the first person to rule from Dunyveg. Around the year 1200, his great-grandson, Somerled of Argyll, took an active part in reconstructing monastic life and buildings on Iona. He was also active in restoring the Western Isles to Gaelic control, for, Viking though he was, he had Gaelic ancestry, and in his own lifetime succeeded in asserting a sort of *de facto* independence for Islay, Mull, and several of the smaller islands. A century and a half later, we find his descendant, MacDonald of Islay, enjoying the title *Lord of the Isles*. For the next century and a half or so, Dunyveg was the seat of power for the Lords of the Isles. When the Lordship was abolished in 1493 there followed a period of chaos and struggle between the dispossessed MacDonalds and the conquering Campbells, until Dunyveg Fell in 1615 and, with it, four and a half centuries of MacDonald rule. The last occupant of the castle, Sir James, was taken prisoner. The MacDonald lands were confiscated and given to their Campbell enemies. From his prison in Edinburgh, Sir James made good his escape, first to his cousins in Ireland – the MacDonalds of Antrim – and later to Spain. In the calmer atmosphere of 1620 he returned to London to enjoy a royal pardon and pension from King James I (VI of Scotland); but there was never any question of regaining Dunyveg or its accompanying lands. When he died in London, his wife and family were in poverty and disappeared from the pages of history. As later happened Walter Frederick Campbell's son after the bankruptcy of his father, John MacDonald, *Ian Lom*, the bard and direct descendant of Somerled, also left a literary legacy to his people – an avalanche of satire and vituperation such as only the Gaelic language is capable of. It is all directed at the Campbell usurper who enjoyed royal protection, who was 'as eloquent as a parrot in his talk,' and who 'filched from us by trickery verdant, lovely Islay and Kintyre with its green plains'.

All during the Viking Era, the Lordship of the Isles, and the age of the Landlords, there stood in the south-east of the island, untouched by the tides and affairs of humankind, a beautifully proportioned and ornamented free-standing stone monument, known the world over as *The Kildalton Cross*. We came upon it suddenly. No doubt it owes its survival to the obscurity of its location. Dating, it is thought, from around the year AD 800, it is not the only cross of note on Islay, much less in all of Scotland, but it is the finest of its kind and the only one totally intact. In its artistic style it is closely related to the Crosses of St John, St Martin and St Oran in Iona.

The free-standing crosses probably evolved from the ancient megalithic Standing Stones. Known as *High Crosses*, their development in Ireland can be traced through three phases. The earliest of them date from around AD 700, and are known as *The Donegal Group*. The second group dates from the ninth and early tenth centuries. These reach the peak of perfection and artistic beauty in the exquisitely ornamented *Scripture Crosses* such as those of Monasterboice, Clonmacnoise and Kells. Then after a lull of about a century and a half, there emerged *the late High Crosses of the twelfth century*. The Celtic church in Scotland evolved its own style in this form of monumental sculpture, but it was also influenced by Irish, Pictish, Viking, and Northumbrian traditions.

The most interesting of the figure carvings on the Kildalton Cross is the sculpture of the Virgin and Child with angels. It bears remarkable similarity to St Oran's Cross in Iona and the Virgin and Child scene in the Book of Kells. Biblical scenes, such as *The Sacrifice of*

Isaac, together with key-patterns and animal and serpent ornamentation, all in high relief, are to be found both on Irish High Crosses
and on that of Kildalton.

So, there for over a thousand years stands *The Kildalton Cross*, silently
inviting repentance and reflection. Considering the political and
social history of the ages, the pilgrim is reminded to have second
thoughts about the pursuit of the transient. Kings, lairds and family
pride, blended whiskeys and single malts, must all be judged ultimately in the light of the cross, that is, in the light of love. St Paul
made such an evaluation in the first century – 'all I want is to know
Christ and him crucified,' and 'we have not here a lasting city but
seek one that is to come.' And in the long winter nights in her
impoverished Blasket Island home in the early twentieth century,
the same truth dawned on the illiterate Peig Sayers: 'I think that
everything is folly except for loving God.'

CHAPTER 7

Applecross
– Maelrubha's Sanctuary

It was Daphne Pochin Mould who introduced me to Applecross –
not the good woman in person, but her books on Celtic matters,
notably, *Scotland of the Saints*. On reading that book, I formed in my
heart a dream that was realised in July 1994. My companions and I
made our pilgrim approach from Inverness via the low-key loveliness of Strath Bran. Taking a left turn at Kinlochewe, we drove at
our usual leisurely pace skirting Glendocherty on the left. Before
reaching Torridon village, I thought my heart and mind would
burst in an attempt to absorb the extraordinary natural beauty that
was opening up with every twist and turn of the road. Rarely have I
seen anything so entrancing. There was something about the text-
ure of the light, first on the mountains, then on the lake – Upper
Loch Torridon – which, under the influence of the evening sunshine, presented itself as a golden mirror. As if the general scene
were not overwhelming enough, there were, too, the haunting
underwater reflections which left me – not without pain, it must be
said – at the edges of finitude, because the beauty of the scene could
neither be adequately contained nor expressed.

We stopped by a little church and ancient graveyard, which in far
off times some Celtic monk may well have designated 'the place of
his resurrection'. We prayed there for a while. And then, continuing
to feast our eyes on the unfolding scene, motored on. By the time
we reached Shieldaig, driving proved impossible once more; the
scene called for pause and silent contemplation. So there we sat on
the edge of Loch Shieldaig, with Loch Torridon beyond, and
beyond that the waters of the North Minch and beyond that again
the Isle of Lewis, and beyond that everything that the Celtic imagi-
nation is capable of creating, even to *Tír na nÓg* and heaven itself.
The sheer beauty was almost enticing us away from the goal of our

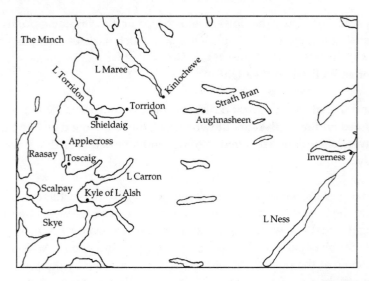

pilgrimage which was the monastic site of St Maelrubha at Applecross.

The Applecross peninsula, which lies between Loch Torridon and Loch Carron, is mountainous and sparsely populated. The village of the same name is on its west coast and there are alternative routes, the one by the ancient mountain pass of *Bealach na Ba* (The Pass of the Cows), and the other by way of the new (1977) coast road. Strangers to both, we opted for the latter and were treated to yet another scenic spectacle. At first we enjoyed and commented on the woodland scenery. Gradually silence descended as we navigated one hair-pin bend after another, careful not to look too closely to the right where the cliffs and man-made earthworks fell all too precipitously towards the great wide sea. Again we stopped. And again we prayed. This was a day to remember. Finally, we reached the *mons gaudi*, and producing the cameras, proceeded to picture the little harbour and village of Applecross gleaming under the last rays of the setting sun.

Not having a camper's guide, we had journeyed in the hope that there would be a camp-site. There was. It was getting late and the deer were down from the hills for their twilight grazing as we pitched our tents. Despite our tiredness, retiring to bed was not the thing to do on such a balmy evening. We walked in the direction of

Toscaig, admiring the flowers and shrubs in the wayside gardens, pausing to savour the deep silence and watch darkness creep over the waters. It was with much satisfaction that we ate our picnic supper and retired for the night.

And then it rained. But it didn't just rain. It rained and rained and rained and rained! At about two o'clock the following day, like the raven leaving the ark, I ventured out and reported back that it was dry.

That was the signal for all to search for dry clothes in the car and raid the boot for something to eat. In no time at all we were attending to matters of the spirit and set out to discover where St Maelrubha had established his 'place of resurrection'. A kindly woman at the post office told me that it was down by the present parish church – Presbyterian – at no great distance from where we were standing. Again, it was easy to slip into a prayerful mood as we stood there on the hallowed ground with the islands of Raasay and Skye forming a picturesque background to the sea which lapped at our feet. There is now no recognisable trace of the early mediaeval monastic foundation, but within the parish church there are three ornamented stone fragments of high crosses or memorial slabs dating from about the eighth century.

And who, one may legitimately ask, was this Maelrubha of Applecross? He was many faceted: a seventh-century Irish Pict, of the same blood as Colmcille, and – if we are to believe the chronicler – a cousin of St Comgall who founded the renowned monastery of Bangor in Co Down. According to the *Annals of Tighernach*, Maelrubha was born in Co Derry on January 3, AD 642, and at an early age entered the monastery of Bangor, where, according to some accounts – not wholly reliable ones, it must be said – he soon became the abbot, only to resign his post after a few years and sail away for Alba's shore. The year was AD 671. It would seem that he worked for about two years in Kintyre and Dal Riada generally before making his principal foundation at Applecross. It was a well-chosen spot, sufficiently fertile and open to the sunshine, at the mouth (*Aber*) of the Crossan river[1] – *Abhainn Maelrubha*, Maelrubha's river, as it is known in Gaelic. By the thirteenth century the name

Aber-Crossan had been transmuted into the very English sounding *Applecross*.

Although a century after Colmcille and Moluag, Maelrubha's personal missionary work and the continuing influence of Applecross had a major impact on the Christianisation of Scotland and would have been even more significant had not the Viking raids begun so soon after its foundation in AD 673. Maelrubha, who was abbot for fifty-one years, enjoyed such a reputation for holiness and miracles that he was adopted as patron of the entire North West. There is a tradition in Scotland that he was martyred, but this seems to have originated from confusion with another saint. The most reliable sources indicate that he died at Applecross on 21 April, AD 722, aged eighty. Under that date, the *Martyrology of Tallaght* has the following entry:

In Alba, in purity,
After forsaking all comforts,
Has gone from us with his mother,
Our brother, Maelrubha.

The saint's death did not break the links with Ireland nor with Bangor. The above mentioned *Annals of Tighernach* record a boating accident in AD 737 which resulted in the death of Abbot Failbhe of Applecross and twenty-two of his monks. *The Annals of Ulster*, which mention the same tragic event, also record the death in AD 801 of Oigi of Applecross, Abbot of Bangor.

With the exception of Colmcille, Maelrubha became the best known saint in Scotland, although, as O'Hanlon notes, his name 'is made up of consonants, apt to be liquefied. It occurs in many transmutations, such as in Mulruby, Malruf, Malrou, Molroy, Malrew, Mulruy, Melriga, Marow, Morow, Marrow, Morew, Maro, Maroy, Murruy, Mareve; also in Arrow, Erew, Errew, and Olrou. A further retrenchment discards the first element of the compound name, and gives Rice, Row, Ro, Rufus, Ruvius; and, to crown all, the natives on the east side of Scotland combine both his name and title. Thus, they run "St Malrubhe" into the euphonistic forms of Summaruff, Samarive, Samarevis, Samerivis, Samarivis, Samarvis, Smarevis, Smarivis, Samaravis, and Sumereve.' (see: O'Hanlon, *Lives of the Irish Saints*, IV, pp 257-258).

As well as those in Dal Riada, there are many dedications to St Maelrubha throughout western and northern parts of the country – Skye, Lewis, Western Ross, Cromarty, and the Black Isle among them. There is one, however, that stands out from all the rest, and that is a small island in Loch Maree, appropriately named *Inis Maree* – Maelrubha's Island. This must have been our saint's retreat, his hide-out, comparable to Colmcille's 'remote place in the wilderness' and Cuthbert's Farne Island cell. A little graveyard and part of the monastic vallum survive, but the holy well, so long a Mecca for the mentally ill, has been filled in.

When Maelrubha died, a zone of six miles around the monastery at Applecross was declared a Sanctuary or place of refuge, where criminals might escape the rigours of the law if they could reach it without being apprehended. The Sanctuary was defined by a series of monoliths of which none remain. The Vikings plundered the monastery but didn't live long to enjoy their booty because their ship sank within sight of the shore as they departed.

Despite the ravages of time, Applecross remained alive until the Reformation. After that cataclysmic event only a scatter of fragments and memories survive from this once inspiring monastery: Maelrubha's Seat, Maelrubha's River, Maelrubha's Island, Maelrubha's Cell, and *Claidh* Maelrubha (Maelrubha's grave), where two round stones near the chapel are said to mark his grave. The ornamented High Cross fragments preserved in the parish church are also relics of the days when Applecross was a beacon of Christian light for much of Scotland.

The afternoon was brightening as we said goodbye to this lovely spot where 'the tonsured red-headed one' (*Maelrubha*) awaits the resurrection. In a final spurt of bravery, instead of returning by the coast road, we faced the car towards *Bealach na Ba*, and after six miles of demanding and careful mountain driving, we found ourselves over two thousand feet above the sea, wide-eyed and speechless yet again at the beauty all around.

Notes
1. I have not yet found a satisfactory meaning for 'Crossan' in the name 'Abercrossan'. It may mean 'the estuary of the razor-bills' (*crosán*), or it may refer to the monastic High Cross/es (*crois/eanna*).

CHAPTER 8

On Pilgrimage to Lindisfarne

The name Lindisfarne is probably best known today as being the birth-place of a wonderful manuscript known as *The Lindisfarne Gospels*. This extraordinary book, the product of an Irish monastic foundation in the process of making a difficult transition to Saxon control, is one of the most precious treasures of Britain today. To view the book, however, one does not go to Lindisfarne off the Northumbrian coast, but to the Department of Manuscripts at the British Library, which owns it. It wasn't the making of the book that was my prime interest in setting out on pilgrimage to Lindisfarne, but the pioneers who, as it were, made the island – and the book.

The pilgrimage to Lindisfarne was a three day event. Leaving Dundalk, in the late afternoon, we took the ten o'clock sailing from Larne and spent the night in Stranraer. Next morning we drove to Portpatrick to commemorate the famine-Irish who, in the nineteenth century, had crossed the short sea route in great numbers, not as pilgrims but as refugees from a regime of horror, starvation and death. From this landing place men, women and little children walked barefoot a hundred miles and more, seeking work in factory and farm. And yet, these barefooted beggars were pilgrims indeed, and missionaries as well, their coming making a significant difference to post Reformation Scotland. For example, in 1791 there was only one person known to be a Catholic in the region of Barrhead-Nitshill-Pollockshaws. Now there are five Catholic parishes.

The next pause was at Kirkmadrine to view the early Christian ornamented stones – all that remains of a strong settlement and possibly the diocesan capital of the area in times after St Ninian. After the scenic drive by Luce Bay, we came to the Isle of Whithorn and Whithorn itself. It was at the Catholic church here that Pope

John Paul II celebrated the Eucharist during his 1982 visit, so what better could I do than follow his example.

Coming from Dundalk, we could not but be conscious of the reputed missionary work of St Edana in the ancient kingdom of Galloway. This Irish nun is best known as Moninne in Dundalk itself and the surrounding counties of Down, Armagh, Monaghan and Louth. According to tradition, before going to Scotland, she lived for a time in the Carlingford area of the Cooley Peninsula, later had a cell on Faughart Hill, and later still had her 'desert' at the foot of Slieve Gullion in south Armagh, where the ruins of a little oratory may still be seen at Killeevy (*cill shléibhe* – the mountain chapel). *The Annals of Ulster* record her death as having taking place on 6 July, AD 516. Under that date, too, St Aengus gives her the following notice in his *Féilire*:

> Moninde of Slieve-Gullion,
> A beautiful pillar;
> A bright pure victory she gained,
> The sister of Muire-Mary.

And if the annals are correct in recording her death in AD 516, then she, like St Brigid, is one of those outstanding saintly people who flourished between the time of St Patrick and rise of the great monastic communities of the sixth century. The reference to her in the *Féilire* as being a sister of Mary the Mother of God is an indication of the esteem in which she was held in mediaeval times.

Because of the prefixing of the name *Edana* with the Irish honorific and endearing *'mo'* (my), her name appears in a variety of forms: Moninne in the north-eastern parts of Ireland, Modenna, Moninna, Moninde, Medana, Edana, in south-west Scotland. Her chief religious foundation is said to have been Chilnecase in Galloway, but her name survives in many place-names, among them: Maidens, Kirkmaiden, Maiden Castle, and of course, Edinburgh, where her sanctuary was a pilgrim shrine long before King Edwin's day.

Leaving behind Galloway of the Irish, we continued through Castle Douglas with its multi-million pound cattle trade, *via* Locherbie and Langholm. With the Cheviot Hills to the left and Tweedsmuir to the

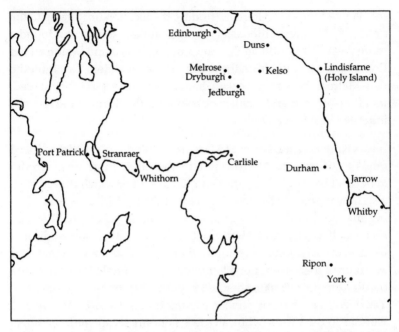

right the landscape became more wooded and undulating. The Border Forests cover about 14% of the land in this area, providing well over 100,000 tonnes of timber annually. But the day was far spent and we kept a steady eye on Old Melrose as a destination of no mean interest to pilgrims bound for Lindisfarne. As I had no accurate memory of the site of Old Melrose from a previous visit made in 1969, we settled for the night in the lovely simple campsite within the picturesque town of Melrose itself, and found it to be, in all our experience in Scotland, the cheapest and best suited to our needs.

The story of Melrose (as distinct from *Old* Melrose) is rooted in the twelfth century when St Bernard of Clairvaux established a community of Cistercian monks at Rievaulx in Yorkshire in the north of England under the abbotship of Blessed William, a disciple of Bernard himself. Rievaulx's most illustrious abbot is undoubtedly St Aelred, one of the first Englishmen to join the community, and its most famous daughter-house is Melrose Abbey, founded just five years after the establishment of Rievaulx. The new community first settled at Old Melrose, superceding the humble Celtic foundation which had predated it by over half a thousand years. But in 1136, the 'White Monks of Melrose,' finding the location unsuitable to the needs of a Cistercian monastery and apostolate, sought and found a more suitable location on the banks of the Tweed and beside an old Roman road leading from the south to Scotland. Here they built the new Melrose, here they worked, here they prayed. Here they stayed, too, for over four and a half centuries until the death of the last disinherited monk in AD 1590.

It was King David I, son of St Margaret of Scotland, who introduced monks not only to Melrose but to the other three great border abbeys – Dryburgh, Jedburgh and Kelso – all of which played such a significant part in the development of the Scottish Lowlands during the late Middle Ages. Despite spoliation by Edward II (1322), Richard II (1385), and Hertford (1545), the gifted and dedicated Cistercians of Melrose restored their splendid abbey again and again until there were none left to do so. The final blow came with the Reformation (1560), soon after which the community died out. Yet, even in its present ruinous condition, it is a source of awe and wonder to the visitor who can view not only its splendid architectural features but detect the devotion and sense of humour present in those artistic monks who have left us in stone the ornamented gargoyles, the Coronation of the Virgin Mary, the angelic musicians and even the pig playing the bagpipes!

Beautiful though it is, Melrose Abbey was not allowed to divert us from our determination to find its predecessor, Old Melrose. Nor could the temptations of Abbotsford, with its memories of Sir Walter Scott, nor the archaeological discoveries at Trimontium, a frontier post and Roman headquarters in the fourth century. After some search and inquiry we found Old Melrose unmarked and down a long private road, on both sides of which were displayed all the beauty of a woodland in summer sunshine. Eager to absorb all that the lovely day and location had to offer, I spotted a man seated comfortably in front of his house and engaged him in conversation. It didn't take long to discover that we were birds of a feather. He expressed a desire to visit the ancient capital at Tara in central Ireland, and went on to discuss the mythological battle of Moy Tura, said to have been fought in the West of Ireland some time during the latter half of the first millennium BC. (We are told that the combatants were two rival branches of the *Tuatha De Danann* (the fairies) and their engagement is still celebrated in that jaunty Irish melody *Sí Beag, Sí Mór*, The Little Fairies & The Big Fairies.) Having gone on to talk about some other matters of mutual interest, we ended up discussing the various kinds of energies found at some old and modern monastic sites and buildings.

The name 'Melrose' – *Maol Ros* (the smooth promontory) – is derived from the local topography wherein the river Tweed loops around three sides of a spit of land. At the actual site of Old Melrose there is a refurbished estate house, now converted into rented apartments. Aside from a slightly elevated area, there is nothing to indicate the location of this once thriving Celtic monastery which was founded from Lindisfarne by St Aidan, and first ruled by his disciple and close friend, the Anglo-Saxon abbot Eata. This was the spot where the youthful Cuthbert, a shepherd boy off the Lammermour Hills, came in AD 651 seeking admittance as an aspirant monk, and where inAD 664 he read St John's gospel to his dying friend and prior, St Boisil.

In AD 839, the Dalriadic Scots invaded the area and destroyed the monastery. Later, a little community of strict-observance Celtic monks known as 'the friends of God' – *Ceilí Dé*, or *Culdees* – made their home there. In post-Reformation polemical works, attempts have often been made to present the Culdees as belonging to an early Christian Scottish tradition independent of Rome. But modern scholarship makes it abundantly clear that they were the product of the eighth-century Celtic monastic reform spearheaded by St Mael Ruan from his monastic foundation at Tallaght, Co Dublin. After the Culdee phase, there was a chapel dedicated to St Cuthbert at Melrose, and then came the Cistercians.

In the communion of saints we saluted them all, joined them in praise of our common Heavenly Father, and took our leave of the hallowed spot.

At this point there was nothing between us and Lindisfarne except mileage. We drove straight to Berwick-on-Tweed and took the Newcastle road south as far as Beal, which is the turn-off point for the island. Tidal conditions were favourable – Lindisfarne is a tidal island – so we sped across the three or more miles of causeway through the sands to our pilgrim destination. As the day was sunny and warm we started with a picnic, after which we surveyed the island and walked most of it. After that it was down to the details and entering more thoroughly into the spirit of this holy place.

The island of Lindisfarne, or Holy Island as it is now more frequently called, first came into prominence in AD 635. The country had been through centuries of turbulence. The Britons, who were in possession of so much of it from pre-historic times, were subjected first to the Roman conquest, then to an unnerving stream of Irish raids from the west, and finally, to the biggest invasion of all, when across the British Channel and North Sea swept hoards of Teutonic Saxons, Angles, Jutes and other savages who overran much of the country and virtually demolished whatever civilisation and Christianity lay before them. But, as always, the passage of time, combined with human resilience, began once more to have a beneficial effect. It was at this turning point that Lindisfarne entered history.

Oswald, the Saxon king of Northumbria, didn't have a smooth passage to his throne. When his father was killed in AD 617, both he and his brother Oswy fled to Dal Riada and found refuge in Iona where they were both converted to Christianity. Later, when Oswald regained his father's lost kingdom, he sent a plea to Iona for missionaries. Iona responded quickly but the monk chosen to lead the mission – Corman by name – was not flexible enough for such a diplomatic venture. St Adamnán says that he soon returned to his monastery and informed his superiors at a meeting that 'he could make nothing of the Angles, that they were a race of untamable savages, and of a stubborn and barbarous spirit'. At that same meeting, another monk, Aidan, spoke up and calmly said to him: 'It seems to me, my brother, that you have been too hard upon these ignorant people: you have not, according to the apostolic counsel, offered them first the milk of gentle doctrine, to bring them by degrees, while nourishing them with the Divine Word, to the true understanding and practice of the more advanced precepts.' In the event, Aidan himself was chosen to launch a second Northumbrian mission. He was ordained bishop at Iona and sent upon his way, not only by Seghen, his abbot and fourth successor to Colmcille, but with the goodwill and prayers of the whole community.

The year of his arrival, AD 635, is a date of the greatest significance in English church history. His friend and patron, King Oswald, gave him great latitude in choosing a suitable location for his new monastic foundation, but instead of opting for good land and prosperous surroundings, Aidan, true to his Celtic tradition, chose the tidal island of Lindisfarne as the centre of operations. Across the water was the royal residence of Bamburg. King and bishop held each other in high regard and worked well together. In the initial stages of his missionary endeavour, Aidan did not understand the language of the Northumbrians, but the king, being fluent in Irish from his Iona days, acted as interpreter. How impressive it must have been for so many people to see this young, energetic Saxon king translating for his people the Word of God as announced by an Irish bishop. Sadly, this deep friendship and joint apostolic endeavour of the saintly king and bishop were brought to a violent end after only seven years. In AD 642, at the age of thirty eight, Oswald died while fighting the heathen Penda of Mercia. His scull, having been exposed on a stake for a considerable time, was rescued by his brother Oswy and received reverently by Aidan. His hands, which had met a like fate, were taken to the royal stronghold at Bamburg and placed in a silver casket. Oswald was venerated as a saint and martyr.

Aidan's first church in his new mission field was at the chosen monastic site on Holy Island. Though the little wooden building with its thatched roof has long since disappeared, archaeologists have identified and staked out what they consider to be the exact site. To stand on this spot, which is now within the priory church ruins, was for me the highlight of my pilgrimage to Lindisfarne. That humble little house of worship was superceded by others over the centuries following until, after the Norman conquest, the Benedictine monks at Durham acquired Lindisfarne as a sub-priory, and at the end of the eleventh century began building the priory church which, even in its present ruinous state, is an imposing monument.

St Aidan was succeeded in the see of Lindisfarne by another Iona monk, an Irishman named Finan. It was during his episcopate that a monastic foundation was made at Whitby, where, under the Abbess Hilda, the community acquired and retained a reputation for learning, holiness and good works.

It was about this time, too, that the infamous 'Paschal Controversy' began to come to the boil.

Looking back now, it all seems like a bottle of smoke. How could a difference over such a minor issue as how to calculate the date of Easter generate such long-lasting and sundering bitterness? Was it not, after all, more a matter of astronomy and mathematics than of faith and morals? Indeed it was, but it became the focal point of party, racial and personal tensions that had been building up for years.

The party tensions were the constantly recurring ones between 'progressives' and 'conservatives.' The progressives in this case wanted to impose the up-to-date method of calculating the date of Easter recently adopted in Rome. The conservatives wished to retain the older Roman method long practised in the Celtic church.

The racial tensions had been building up as the missionary thrust of the church in the south of England (a thrust begun by St Augustine of Canterbury in AD 597, the year of Colmcille's death) penetrated further north and increasingly interacted with the southwards spreading Celtic church from the north.

The personal elements show most clearly in the behaviour of Wilfrid, Abbot of Ripon, at the Synod of Whitby in 664, where the whole issue was finally thrashed out. With his fundamentalist interpretation of Jesus giving the keys of the kingdom of heaven to St Peter, Wilfrid carried the day at the Synod, but the trauma of it all lingered for centuries. Indeed it still angers the Celt to read in Bede about the behaviour of Wilfrid who had, at the age of fourteen, been accepted into the monastic life at Lindisfarne and, having been educated there, got the necessary permission and backing of bishop Finan and the community for further studies on the Continent and at Rome. It turned out to be a case of putting a beggar on horseback. Returning home with a head full of conceit and arrogance, Wilfrid proceeded at the Synod of Whitby to round on his Celtic benefactors, publicly humiliating and ridiculing Bishop Colman and his delegates as well as pouring scorn on Colmcille and casting doubts on his holiness. Whatever about the personal insults hurled at himself, Colman was deeply hurt by the slur cast on St Colmcille. Nevertheless he did not retaliate. He quietly placed the facts as he knew them before the delegates and let them make up their own minds. King Oswy, who presided over the gathering, opted for the more modern system of calculating Easter and the majority of the delegates fell in line with him.

Curiously, in view of what happened in England almost a thousand years later, a major factor in bringing an urgency to the resolution of the controversy was the king's marital problems. The king, who had been converted by the Irish monks, followed the old Roman or Celtic method of calculating the date of Easter, but his Kentish wife followed the new Roman system introduced into England by St Augustine of Canterbury. At that time Christian married couples were expected to abstain from marital intimacy as part of Lenten penance. But due to the discrepancy in calculating Easter, partners to a marriage could find themselves abstaining not just for the standard forty days but for anything up to ten weeks, and this was proving a considerable strain not only in the royal kitchen but in the royal bedchamber!

After the synod, Lindisfarne and the Northumbrian church entered a new phase and the Irish influence waned, but not immediately. St Colman resigned his see, collected his few belongings and returned to Iona with those Irish and Saxon monks who were not happy with the post-Whitby arrangement. He left St Eata, his former pupil and friend, now abbot of the daughter-house at Melrose, to take on the care of Lindisfarne as well. St Tuda, another Irishman, was appointed to fill the vacant see. Tuda lived only few months. He was struck down by the *Buí Chonaill*, the Yellow Plague, in that same year of AD 664 and died at Durham.

Meanwhile, Colman considered his future in the calm friendly atmosphere of Iona. He and his followers chose to go to Ireland, taking with them the bones of St Aidan which they had brought from Holy Island. Having established a new monastery on Inisbofin off the Galway coast, Colman continued to live a life of holiness and austerity until his death on 8 August, AD 676. During his abbotship he established a separate monastery on the mainland for the Saxon members of the community. Some dissension had arisen between the two races, due apparently to the fact that when the good weather came in early summer the Celtic monks were in the habit of taking to their boats, leaving the Saxons at home to do the donkey-work in the fields.

Any Lindisfarne pilgrimage is incomplete without giving thought to St Cuthbert, whom we have already referred to in relation to Melrose. His birth-place has been claimed for England, Scotland and Ireland, but the question remains open, though the weight of tradition and historical sources seems to favour Ireland. Some authors go so far as to identify him with the province of Leinster, more specifically with the Kells area of Co Meath, or Kilmacud in Dublin. However an absolute claim for any of the three countries is still impossible. Like Bede, many writers avoid the issue, and since each of the contending nations might well rejoice in having such a wonderful saint as their own, the historical vagueness surrounding his birthplace leaves us all in with a chance.

After Whitby, the Saxon abbot Eata transferred Cuthbert from Ripon to be his deputy in Lindisfarne. The task ahead was daunting. Morale in the monastery was at a low ebb. There was a lot of healing and up-building to be done, and Cuthbert was the man for it. A few years after the immediate fall-out from Whitby, Eata was appointed to the see of Lindisfarne. There he could see for himself what a wonderful rebuilding of monastic life and morale had gone on under Cuthbert.

Because of his life-long dedication to prayer and contemplation, it is not surprising to find Cuthbert taking on the life of a hermit at various times. About the year AD 676 he set up a hermitage for himself on the tiny tidal-island which is only a stone's throw from the monastery and now known as *St Cuthbert's Island*. This location proved altogether too convenient for people seeking him out, so he moved to the innermost of the Farne Islands. However he was not allowed peace and quiet for very long as he found himself elected Bishop of Lindisfarne when Eata was transferred to Hexham. This office he filled faithfully for two years but, finding his health failing, he celebrated his last Christmas at Lindisfarne in AD 686 and, hav-

ing retired once more to the Inner Farne hermitage, he gave up his
spirit to the Lord on March 20, AD 687. His body, which was buried
in Lindisfarne, was found to be incorrupt after eleven years and so
it remained. After many translations it rested in the cathedral at
Durham from the tenth century until the Reformation. In 1537, the
agents of Henry VIII rifled the shrines of Durham, at which time the
body of the saint was removed to a secret place, known only, it is
said, to some members of the English Benedictines.

Interesting as all of this might be, my own interest in Cuthbert is as
an itinerant preacher, a 'missioner'. Woven into Bede's accounts of
his miracles, his austerities, his managerial capacities, his diplomacy,
and all the rest, is a portrait of Cuthbert the missioner. He is presented as travelling about the borders of Scotland and England and
throughout Northumbria, talking to rich and poor, visiting homes,
dropping in to see an old woman who had been mother to him in
bygone days, preaching to the ordinary people, giving nuns'
retreats, renewing the faith, celebrating the sacraments, encourag-
ing and instructing people in prayer, comforting them in their trials
and griefs, and all the while trying to keep his own relationship
with God nourished and healthy. This is *my* Cuthbert, because this
is also my life, however pale an imitation it may be of that of the
great man himself. It is because of Cuthbert I went to Lindisfarne,
and because of Aidan, whose mission life was of a similar nature. In
God's good time, and with his help, I'll go there on pilgrimage
again to drink once more from the well-springs of grace.

CHAPTER 9

That Genius Dunce

The Outer Hebrides are so rich in hallowed sites that it is difficult to choose a specific location or shrine for pilgrimage. The *Western Isles*, as they are now termed by the postal service, are about five hundred in number and there's a story or two and a saint or two associated with most of them.

Mingulay has a Celtic monastic site dating from early mediaeval times. Barra has St Finbarr and the footings of a beehive cell said to have been that of St Brendan the Navigator. Eriskay was the birthplace of Donald-Mac-Iain-Vich-Hamish, a Samson-like warrior who defeated a vastly superior force at the battle of Carinish in AD 1601. It was also where Bonnie Prince Charlie first landed in '45; and the same island saw the sinking of *The Politician* in 1941, freighted with crates of *uisge beatha* – a godsend to the thirsty islanders and the basis for Compton MacKenzie's book *Whiskey Galore!* South Uist has a monastic site associated with St Donan, as well as Flora MacDonald's birthplace, a missile-testing site, and probably the tallest statue of the Virgin and Child in the world. On Benbecula – *the island of the small bare hill* – Donald-Allan MacIsaac took me on a tour of a Columban site, and later, pointing to a grassy mound between road and sea, remarked with emphasis: 'That's the spot where St Cormac the Sailor first taught us the Christian Faith.' The little isle of Grimsay boasts the ruins of St Michael's Chapel, the legacy, it is said, of the saintly Lady Amie, heiress of Loarn and estranged wife of John of Islay. North Uist has Trinity College, and Berneray is proud of Donald Macleod, alias *'The Old Trojan'*, a veteran of the '45, who married three times and had twenty children by the first wife, none by the second and nine by the third. His third bride was eighteen while he himself was pushing eighty. He died at the age of one hundred and three – the headstone only credits him with ninety – when his youngest child was only nine. St Clement's,

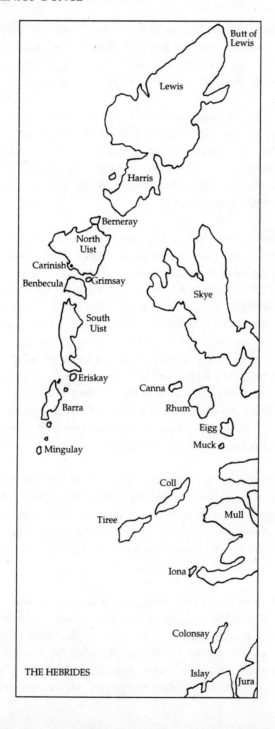

THE HEBRIDES

at Rodel in Harris, is keeper of his bones. Lewis has the Callanish Standing Stones, and an ancient church site dedicated to St Maelrubha at the Butt of Lewis. And this listing gives only a handful of possible places to which the pilgrim might make tracks.

For myself, I have visited many of the places named above as I have worked on missions throughout the islands and grown to love the people who are so warm, friendly and still possessed of the Gaelic language and culture, albeit in a somewhat weakened state, partly due to historical factors, but chiefly to the present all-pervasive influence of the English language.

On pilgrimage, however, I made my way on a stormy winter's day to the remote Atlantic side of Barra where, at the head of a tiny sandy bay, an old graveyard encloses a ruined cell, said to be that of St Brendan. On the same island I made another pilgrimage to St Columba's Well; and on St Patrick's Day, 1992, amid storm and rain, I climbed *Bealach a'Dhágain* – 'Fr Duggan's Way' – a mountain pass of a thousand feet which the seventeenth-century Limerick Vincentian missionary used to take on his way to celebrate the Eucharist on a Mass-rock for his persecuted flock. It gave me a small personal experience of what the man must have regularly endured, for I got soaked to the skin, fell several times, and with squelching shoes and aching back, and generally the worse for wear, returned to my presbytery base at Northbay.

Despite the colour and romance associated with so many of the above mentioned places and personalities, my choice for a specific pilgrimage – rather than a mere visit – fell on *Teampull na Trionad*, 'Church of the Trinity,' and Trinity College at Carinish in North Uist – a place to which my ever helpful friend, Duncan MacLellan of Kyles Flodda, introduced me.

Little remains now of this once great school where the MacVurich bards taught and where, according to a strong local tradition, the outstanding mediaeval Franciscan theologian, John Duns Scotus, pursued some of his early studies. As with my other winter pilgrimages in the Outer Hebrides, the outing to Trinity College was on a wild, cold day. I climbed the grassy slopes once occupied by the illustrious seat of learning. The few remaining walls were not even built in the days when its most famous pupil was having crowns of thorns and wreaths of glory thrust upon his brow at the universities of Oxford and Paris.

Of his life before ordination to the priesthood, we know nothing with any certainty of John Scotus, not even his nationality. In early mediaeval times the word 'Scotus' meant an Irishman, while in late mediaeval times it meant a Scotsman; but there were about two centuries of transition during which the term could indicate either, and it is towards the end of this period that John Scotus lived. The insertion of the qualifier 'Duns' must surely associate him with the Berwickshire town of that name. Nevertheless, the closest we can come to any knowledge about his young life is the strong local tradition regarding his studies here in the Gaelic world of thirteenth-century North Uist.

When John steps onto the pages of history it is as a newly ordained Franciscan priest in Northampton. The date is March 17, 1291. For the next sixteen years he was back and forth between the universities of Oxford and Paris, studying, lecturing, developing his theological opinions. After he had propounded a mature and solidly based theology of Mary the Mother of God at Paris in 1307, tempers ran so high that his life was under threat. For safety, his superiors transferred him to Cologne where he continued to lecture until his untimely death on November 8 of the following year, aged about forty-three. He was buried in the Franciscan church in Cologne. John's holiness was recognised from early on, but it was not until March 20, 1993, that Pope John Paul II declared him 'Blessed' and presented him to the world at large as a man to be imitated, one who produced in his life the virtues of the ultimate model of sanctity, Jesus Christ.

Sixteenth-century humanists and reformers in England mocked the disciples of Duns Scotus as enemies of learning, and referred to them disparagingly as 'Dunses,' from which came the term 'dunce' meaning a dullard or stupid person. Time has shown where the dunce's cap rightly belongs!

John Duns Scotus wove all human knowledge into a wonderful

web of unity, the source of which he saw as a God whose name and nature is Love. If St Francis of Assisi was a living image of that love lived out, his disciple John Duns Scotus was the man who supplied the philosophical and theological theory which gives intellectual shape to it all. John lived by what he preached and his own holiness ever shone through.

Scotus gave a beautiful answer to the question as to why God the Son became man. He did so to redeem and save us, yes, but does that imply that if we hadn't sinned there would be no Incarnation, no baby in the manger, no Son of God walking the world doing good and making God visible in human form? For Scotus, God always intended his Son to become man even if sin had never happened. God loved the world so much that he intended his Son's Incarnation to be the crowning glory of it all. So, over hundreds and thousands of years, God gradually prepared humanity to bring forth his Son in human form. Eventually, under God's grace, the human race comes to a peak of readiness in a young girl called Mary. Mary is so utterly open to God that his grace is able to fill every corner of her being: she is 'full of grace'. Humanity, at its best in her, is ready to bring forth the Son of God.

Scotus remains an influential and inspiring figure in philosophy and theology. Gerard Manley Hopkins, the Jesuit poet, indebted to Scotus in countless ways, said movingly of him, 'Of all men, (he) most sways my spirits to peace.' What a magnificent tribute! And not a bad epitaph – for a 'dunce!'

CHAPTER 10

The Pilgrim Tradition

While I was conducting a parish mission in the heart of Co Cork a series of events took place that set me thinking about pilgrimage as a way of prayer. A little boy of ten took a drink from a soft drinks bottle. Unfortunately the bottle did not contain a soft drink. Instead, it contained paraquat, a deadly weedkiller. There was pandemonium. The distraught parents had him rushed to hospital in Cork. Word of the tragedy spread like gorse-fire throughout the closely-knit community. Shock levels ran high. But what made the occasion so memorable for me were the ensuing events.

Some miles away, at the foot of the mountains near Ballyvourney village, there is a shrine to an early Christian Celtic saint named Gobnait. The shrine is a popular pilgrim destination from time-immemorial. So the shocked community neither sat under the pall of sadness that hung over them, nor waited helplessly for each new word from the hospital. Instead, in a totally spontaneous gesture, virtually every man, woman and child in the area set out on pilgrimage to St Gobnait's shrine. Not only that, many of them spent nights in vigil there as well. The fact that before the next weekend the little boy had resumed his place in the congregation at the mission was a source of great joy and, in the eyes of many, a miracle too; but miracle or no, I was left contemplating this phenomenon of pilgrimage as a powerful expression of what is deepest in humanity.

My reflections led me to delve more deeply into the idea of pilgrimage as a way of making a statement of faith and hope in a spirit of love. And the idea is not peculiar to the Celtic peoples. It is common to Christian, Moslem, Jew, Hindu, and every creed and nationality on the face of the earth.

While the Jews celebrated their three great pilgrim festivals of

Passover, Pentecost and Tabernacles, early Christian pilgrimage
focused on the Holy Sepulchre at Jerusalem, the tomb of the
Resurrection. With the passage of time, the tombs of the martyrs
who laid down their lives for the gospel also became places of pilgrimage, the most notable being the tombs of the apostles Peter and
Paul in Rome. Miraculous cures at these holy places increased their
popularity, but other motives also draw people on pilgrimage – the
giving of thanks, the fulfilling of a vow, the need to do penance, the
need to intercede for a loved one, the longing for faith, the hope of
being somehow touched by the Divine at this place of meeting
between heaven and earth.

In the fourth century, when the persecution of the church in the
Roman Empire ended with the Edict of Milan (AD 313), a new era
of pilgrimage opened up. A number of factors combined to nourish
the atmosphere for increased pilgrim traffic to the Holy Land, and
specifically to Jerusalem and the Holy Sepulchre. These included
the reputed finding of the Holy Cross by St Helena, and the building of a basilica at the Holy Sepulchre by her son, Constantine the
Great (d. AD 337). St Jerome, the renowned scripture scholar, gave
the Holy Land a high profile by his presence there for many years
before his death at Bethlehem in AD 420. Another impetus came
from the development of religious life in the deserts of Syria,
Palestine and Egypt. In the late third and early fourth centuries,
word began to filter through to Western Europe that there were in
those regions monastic sites and tombs worthy of pilgrimage.

While Rome never lacked for pilgrims to the tombs of Peter and
Paul, the numbers were as nothing compared with those going to
the Holy Land from the fourth century onwards. Writing to a group
of consecrated virgins who had made the pilgrimage to the Holy
Sepulchre, St Athanasius of Alexandria (d. AD 373) said that they
could remain with Christ by a holy life although they had left the
scene of his earthly life. His contemporary, St Jerome, tried to cool
down an over-emphasis on pilgrimage saying, 'You can reach the
court of heaven just as well from Britain as from Jerusalem.' But it
was St Bernard of Clairvaux in the twelfth century who gave the
ultimate put-down to would-be pilgrims in his monastic community: 'Your cell is Jerusalem!'

Such a remark would have totally frustrated the enthusiastic Irish St Molua (d. c. AD 605) who said to his abbot, 'Unless I see Rome I shall die soon.' A fellow Irish monk was not so enthusiastic, as is evident from a ninth century manuscript gloss which Robin Flower translates thus:

Who to Rome goes
Much labour, little profit knows;
For God, on earth though long you've sought him,
You'll miss at Rome unless you brought him.

Samthan, an eighth-century Irish abbess, was dismissive of pilgrimage on the grounds that God was to be found everywhere and therefore there was no need for her nuns to go overseas to find him. She may have been mindful of the warning given by her contemporary, St Boniface, the English monk and apostle of Germany, that most women while on pilgrimage lost their virtue!

Not only was one's virtue under threat, so was one's life. Mediaeval pilgrimage involved high risks. As early as the fourth century, the Christian community maintained that complete remission of sins was obtained by making a pilgrimage to a martyr's tomb and meditating there. But while the object of the pilgrimage might have been to put one's affairs right with God, the pilgrim was also strongly advised to put matters right with humankind first, because the pilgrimage might well be a journey of no return.

A married man, for example, who intended going on pilgrimage, was expected first to make restitution for any ill-gotten goods, make adequate provision for the support of his wife and family during his absence, and give as generously as possible to the poor, while at the same time retaining enough cash to see him through the long, costly and dangerous journey. Besides, he had to get written authorisation from the bishop, for without this testimonial letter he was liable to be arrested along the route as an adventurer or a bogus pilgrim – and there were many such.

He might also invest in pilgrim dress. This took the form of penitential garb, rounded off by a broad-brimmed hat, a shoulder-strap bag and a good long stout stick tipped with an iron ferrule, his 'pilgrim's staff.' Finally, before departure he would receive a special liturgical blessing and on that occasion it was expected that he would yet again dip into the long stocking and give a donation to the clergy.

With the passage of the centuries places of pilgrimage multiplied. Rome was still new to the Anglo-Saxons and irresistibly attractive to them. At least eight of their kings went there, as well as countless bishops, clergy and laity. So many were they that, in the vicinity of St Peter's, a whole area – the *Vicus Saxonum* or Saxon village – was inhabited exclusively by them.

To pilgrim destinations already mentioned, we may add the tomb of St Martin of Tours (d. c. AD 397) in France, St Patrick's Purgatory in Ireland, Whithorn of St Ninian and Iona of St Columcille in Scotland, Lindisfarne and Durham in the North of England, to name but some. The roads to Compostella in Northern Spain have rarely been deserted since the reputed 'discovery' in the ninth century of the tomb of St James the Apostle. And, since the murder there of Thomas a Becket in 1170, the world and his wife have been flocking to Canterbury. (On reading some of the pilgrimage shenanigans described by Chaucer one can almost hear St Boniface in the background muttering, 'I told you so.') Favourite pilgrim destinations and stop-overs for pilgrims from these islands include such Irish Continental shrines in Germany, France and Italy, as those of St Killian of Wurzburg (d. 689), Fursa of Peronne (d. c. 648), and Frigidian of Lucca (d. c. 588).

Still in the early mediaeval period, the locations of reputed supernatural apparitions were included in the range of pilgrim places. Such are the shrines of St Michael the Archangel at Monte Gargano in Italy, dating from the sixth century, and the spectacular Mont-Saint-Michel in the North of France, dating from the eighth century. Sites associated with apparitions of the Virgin Mary are legion and date from early mediaeval times to the present day.

Pilgrim traffic brought with it the need for roads, bridges, hostels and services of all kinds. Popes, kings, emperors, bishops, religious orders, responded to the best of their ability. The Knights of St

James, for example, were founded to help pilgrims on their way to Compostella. The Knights Templars and the Knights of Malta started out as religious orders dedicated to offering care, defence and general assistance to pilgrims, especially those who were ill or overcome by the hardships of the journey. As well as these, a variety of local confraternities with much the same aims sprang up from the thirteenth century onwards.

Pilgrims travelled by any means available – boat, horse, mule, donkey, foot. Rarely did people go on bare feet in mediaeval times, but there were exceptions. When King Canute The Great of Denmark became King of England, he went barefoot to the tomb of St Cuthbert at Durham to pray to the saint who enjoyed greatest popularity among his new subjects. While Henry VIII of England was still married to his first wife, Catherine of Aragon, he walked barefoot from the Slipper Chapel on the outskirts of Walsingham to the main shrine. There he lit countless votive candles, presented gifts, and offered prayers for a son and heir. St Louis IX, King of France (d. 1270) walked fifteen miles barefoot on the road to Chartres' exquisite Cathedral of Notre Dame. Meanwhile, the Irish were continuing to make the annual penitential pilgrimage – barefooted or on their knees – to the top of the two and a half thousand foot Croagh Patrick in Co Mayo; and from all over the Continent pilgrims came to do penance and pray at St Patrick's Purgatory, a bleak lake-island in Donegal, where the use of footwear was forbidden.

Of all the pilgrim places in Celtic lands the most popular was the 'holy well'. The noted Celtic scholar Charles Plummer estimated that there were about three thousand holy wells in Ireland alone, that is, about two per parish. It was probably the same in Celtic Britain prior to the Reformation. There were, and are, wells associated with cure for headaches, toothaches, sore eyes, infertility, plague, epilepsy, whooping cough, and many more ailments, including insanity. St Maelrubha's well in Isle Maree in the North West Highlands is an example of the last.

Most Celtic pilgrimages involved a vigil, usually the night before the saint's feast. In some instances the vigil meant lying for the night in the holy place, be it in a ruined oratory or on the slab covering a saint's grave. These 'sleeping places' are known in the Celtic pilgrim tradition as *'leabaí na naomh'*, 'beds of the saints', the best known of which are the *'beds'* at Lough Derg. The vigil is still very much part of the pilgrimage to the national shrine of Mary at Knock, in Ireland, as well as being the reason why vast numbers of pilgrims begin climbing Croagh Patrick before dawn.

By the ninth-century, another type of pilgrim was on the move. Law-breakers and trouble-makers such as arsonists, murderers and heretics might have their sentences of excommunication, exile or banishment commuted to an approved pilgrimage. This policy on the part of the church and state had many humane aspects, but gave rise to problems too. One such problem has a humorous side to it, though only in retrospect; at the time it was hardly humorous for the clergy involved with university students of twelfth and thirteenth-century Paris and elsewhere. In those days the penalty for striking or man-handling a cleric was excommunication, a penalty that could only be lifted by the pope in person and so necessitated a journey to Rome. Apparently this proved an irresistible opportunity for many students. You could beat up your most hated clerical teacher, put on a show of repentance, and get community funding for a trip to Rome (that you could not otherwise afford) in order to have your excommunication lifted! A penalty designed to protect clerics was putting them in greater danger. The abuse became so common that eventually the penalty was abolished.

Where the ancient pilgrimage scored strongly over the modern package-tour was in the matter of time. Pilgrims generally did not have a time-scale. Having arrived at Jerusalem, for example, some were so happy at having reached the Holy Sepulchre and made their peace with God that they stayed on for months or even years helping others in need of care and assistance. Some wished that they might die there. Some did. Those who returned home had the problem of convincing their own people that they had, in fact, made the pilgrimage which they claimed to have made. This led to the bringing home of a *'signum'* or symbol of the place they had visited, for example, a palm from the Holy Land (hence, the term *'palmers'*), or a shell from the beach near Compostella. During the persecution of Catholics in Ireland during the seventeenth and eighteenth-centuries, pilgrims returned from St Patrick's Purgatory in Lough Derg with a distinctive carved wooden crucifix popularly known as *A Penal Cross.*

Pilgrims returning from Jerusalem and wishing to retain their fervour developed the devotion of the Way of the Cross in imitation of the actual *Via Crucis* in Jerusalem, so that they could re-live, stage by stage, the painful journey of our Lord to Calvary. Besides, those who would never make the physical journey to Jerusalem might accompany Jesus in spirit as they meditated step by step on his sacred passion.

Pilgrims who happened to visit Lucca in Northern Italy would not only have prayed at the tomb of St Frigidian but noted with interest the art-form at the shrine of the *Volto Santo,* where the dead Christ on the cross was portrayed in a manner known as 'the Gothic slouch.' This art form influenced the sculptors of the *Late High Crosses* of twelfth-century Ireland. The *Volto Santo* is also the model for the crucifix in general use among Catholics down to modern times.

All true pilgrimage involved the twin activities of prayer and penance. In olden times, there was a great deal of penance involved in the very act of making the journey, but when the pilgrim reached the *mons gaudi* (the hill of joy), the high spot from which one first caught sight of the goal, further penance was frequently undertaken. It was at this point in his pilgrimage that a certain Irishman was penitentially climbing the Scala Sancta in Rome on his knees. It seems that a lady in front of him got her dress caught on the heel of her shoe. Unable to disengage it herself, she asked the Irishman to lift up her dress. 'I will not,' he said, 'Sure 'tis for doing that that I'm doing this!'

The standard Celtic ritual at a holy place consisted largely of *doing the rounds,* that is, walking clockwise around the church or well or graveyard or other holy place, reciting a series of prescribed prayers. These prayers generally consisted of a set number of Paters, Aves and Glorias. From late mediaeval times the recitation of one or several Rosaries, with the accompanying meditation on the principal mysteries of the life, death and resurrection of the Lord, was almost always an integral part of the pilgrim's prayer pattern. In the process of *doing the rounds* there might be further rituals aside from walking, for example placing one's arms around a cross, putting one's knees or head into hollowed stones, drinking from the holy well. Physical activity, bodily involvement, is an important feature in Celtic spirituality.

Before leaving the holy place, the pilgrim usually left an *ex voto* – an object, a coin, a gift. In mediaeval times many shrines depended on such offerings and the same may be said of shrines today. War medals are often left at Our Lady of Victories in Paris. At St Anne de Beaupre, in Quebec, I observed an extraordinary number and variety of crutches and other limb-supports happily left behind by pilgrims as a testimony to their being cured. At the Celtic sites in Ireland and Celtic Britain the *ex voto* was more likely to be a rag tied on a thorn bush (*sceach*), or a coin driven into its trunk or perhaps pitched into the holy well – the origin of throwing coins in a fountain? In the Celtic tradition, the rag on the bush or the coin in the well ritualised a letting go or leaving behind of one's ailment or trouble, or indeed one's prejudice or hatred or bitterness. Was it not the French writer and politician, Chateaubriand, who said, 'There was never a pilgrim who did not come back to his village with one less prejudice and one more idea!'

CHAPTER 11

Making a Pilgrimage
Some suggestions and prayers

A pilgrimage is a journey to a holy place for religious motives, nothing more and nothing less. However, in the light of local, universal and Celtic tradition, there are enduring elements that can be identified. As a Catholic Christian, I suggest giving consideration to the following points:

(1) A prayerful preparation.

(2) A spirit of repentance and openness to conversion.

(3) Celebrating the Sacraments of Reconciliation and Holy Eucharist if possible.

(4) Perhaps a vigil before departure, or at the holy place.

(5) Doing the 'rounds' as explained in chapter ten.

(6) Leaving an *ex voto* at the site.

(7) Some form of celebration afterwards, 'letting one's hair down' in a simple joyful way.

(8) Returning home with a stronger determination to follow the way of our Lord Jesus Christ.

As to the kind of prayers suitable for pilgrimage, there is, first of all, spontaneous prayer arising from the heart. There are also set formulae suggested for specific pilgrimages. The Rosary is a standard prayer used by Catholics in 'doing the rounds'. Since the Rosary belongs to the common pre-Reformation tradition, it is being rediscovered and used by some members of other Christian traditions too. These latter have, of course, their own prayer formulae, and for pilgrimage, what could be more appropriate than the use of the Gradual Psalms (Ps 119/120-133/134) which were prayed by our spiritual ancestors on their pilgrim way to Jerusalem.

At the Redemptorist Monastery in Esker, Athenry, in the West of Ireland, pilgrimages take place on Sunday afternoon during the months of May and October. The pilgrims journey through the spacious monastic environs to a variety of sacred sites or 'stations'. They are invited, but not compelled, to make at least part of this journey barefooted. Fr Dick Tobin, CSSR, himself a member of the Esker community, composed the following prayers for use on the pilgrimage, but as they have a universal quality, they are offered here as models for use or adaptation to other pilgrim situations.

Prayer before setting out on pilgrimage

God of all journeys,
Our beginning and our destination,
I hear your voice calling me to set out.
I hear you in my own restlessness and dissatisfaction:
we have not here a lasting city,
so I will arise and go to my Father.

I hear you calling me as you called Abraham and Moses:
'Go into the land which I will show you.'

I hear you in the voice of your Son:
'Come, follow me.'

I set out now in pilgrimage,
leaving aside the clutter and distraction of the world,
to walk in your presence,
to walk in the footsteps of your Son,
to walk in the footsteps of St Patrick
and all the good men and women who have journeyed before me.

I call on Jesus
to light my path and be my good shepherd.
I call on Mary
to guide my steps as she guided her son's.
I call on Patrick and all the saints of Ireland,
to be my companions on the way.
I call on the good people who have lived and prayed in this place down the years
to pray for me now
that I may have strength and heart for the journey.
I gather all my heart and mind into my walking.
I gather all my longing and seeking into my walking.

I gather all my sorrow for sin into my walking.
I gather all my thanksgiving and delight into my walking.
I gather all my sorrow and heartbreak into my walking.
Let my every step be a prayer of all that is in me,
– all that I know and all that is dark and obscure.

Bless the path on which I go.
Bless the earth under my feet.
Bless the friends who walk by my side.

I set out in the name of the Holy Trinity,
Father, Son and Holy Spirit. Amen.

Prayer for the World
(Praise & intercession)

At some stage of the pilgrimage, preferably on a rise of ground, on top of a hill, or on top of a building, look out over the world around – a world of goodness and beauty, a world of rottenness and evil. With all its tensions, stresses, temptations, it is our world, it is God's world, both sinful and graced, a world in need of continuing redemption.

Praise:

God of the infinite spaces – Glory and praise to you.
God of sun, moon and stars – Glory and praise to you.
God of earth, sea and sky – Glory and praise to you.
God of grass and tree and flower – Glory and praise to you.
God of bird and beast and fish – Glory and praise to you.
God of sunshine, wind and rain – Glory and praise to you.
Father and lover of humanity – Glory and praise to you.

Intercession:

We cry to you on behalf of the world
– God of mercy, hear our prayer.
That we may love and care for the earth, sea and air
– God of mercy, hear our prayer.
That we may love and care for all your creatures
– God of mercy, hear our prayer.

That we may love and care for all your people
– God of mercy, hear our prayer.
For those whose humanity is destroyed by hunger
– God of mercy, hear our prayer.
For those whose humanity is destroyed by the abuse of power
– God of mercy, hear our prayer.
For those whose humanity is destroyed by the sins of others
– God of mercy, hear our prayer.

For all who are lost and lonely
– God of mercy, hear our prayer.
For all who are sick and dying
– God of mercy, hear our prayer.
For all who are depressed and despairing
– God of mercy, hear our prayer.
For all whose hearts are broken
– God of mercy, hear our prayer.
For all who have lost the faith
– God of mercy, hear our prayer.
For all who do not know you
– God of mercy, hear our prayer.
For all who are prisoners of addiction
– God of mercy, hear our prayer.
For all who seek you sincerely
– God of mercy, hear our prayer.
For all who seek you in the wrong places
– God of mercy, hear our prayer.
For all who are lost in their own sins
– God of mercy, hear our prayer.
For all who struggle to make peace
– God of mercy, hear our prayer.
For all who struggle to do good
– God of mercy, hear our prayer.
For all who struggle to save others
– God of mercy, hear our prayer.
For all who have power and influence
– God of mercy, hear our prayer.
For all who are powerless and oppressed
– God of mercy, hear our prayer.
For your church in service of the world

– God of mercy, hear our prayer.
For all who are especially dear to our heart
– God of mercy, hear our prayer.

Let us pray.

Father, it is good for us to be here and to lift our arms on behalf
of the world.
We rejoice in it, because it is your beautiful creation.
We weep over it, because it is so full of suffering and tears.
May we always hold it in our hearts
and bring to it the truth and goodness of your Son's gospel.
We pray this through Christ our Lord. Amen.

Prayer at the end of a pilgrimage
(preferably recited in a church)

My thanks to you, Father,
for the pilgrim journey I have undertaken.
My thanks for the strength and heart
to walk in your presence.

My thanks for your supporting love
along the way.
My thanks for rest and peace
now at the end of it all.

Here in your house
may I taste the peace of heaven,
may I taste the joy of being cleansed and forgiven,
may I taste the fulness of your love.

From this day forth
let all my journeys
echo with the meaning of this journey.
Wherever I go
let me bring with me an awareness of your presence
and the joy of your kingdom,
where you live with your Son and Holy Spirit,
one God forever and ever. Amen.

Finit. Amen. Finit.